A CELEBRATION IN PICTURES

THE BRITISH MOTORIST

A CELEBRATION IN PICTURES

THE BRITISH MOTORIST

LORD MONTAGU OF BEAULIEU

Macdonald
Queen Anne Press

A *Queen Anne Press* BOOK

© Lord Montagu of Beaulieu 1987

First published in Great Britain in 1987 by
Queen Anne Press, a division of
Macdonald & Co (Publishers) Ltd
3rd Floor
Greater London House
Hampstead Road
London NW1 7QX

A BPCC plc Company

British Library Cataloguing in Publication Data

Montagu of Beaulieu, Edward Douglas-Scott-
    Montagu, *Baron*
    The British motorist.
    1. Automobile driving—Great Britain—
    History
    I. Title
    796.7′0941   GV1021

    ISBN 0-356-12775-3

Typeset by Clifford-Cooper Ltd,
Farnham, Surrey
Printed and bound in Great Britain by
Purnell Book Production Ltd,
Member of the BPCC Group,
Paulton, Bristol.

Acknowledgements

The publishers would particularly like to thank Greg Strange for his role in the research and preparation of this book.

Picture Credits

All pictures supplied by the National Motor Museum with the following exceptions:

Austin Rover 144, 169, 201; Barnaby's Picture Library 165; BBC Hulton Picture Library 70, 176 (top); Camera Press 162, 183, 188; Ford 50, 78; Jaguar 143; John Kobal Collection 132; Quadrant Picture Library 160, 167, 175, 184, 186, 187, 190; Rex Features 141 (top), 193; Sandwell Metropolitan Borough Council 96 (top); Topham Picture Library 94, 95, 146, 148, 150, 179; TVR 194.

CONTENTS

INTRODUCTION

This book is all about the British and their love affair with their best friend, the motor car. Like all friendships, it has had its ups and downs; there have been moments of great joy shared together, and equally there have been those times when friends fall out, seemingly without hope of reconciliation. But despite the vicissitudes, and even though the honeymoon may be over, the two in truth remain the best of friends — aware of each other's faults and failings — yet prizing virtues above shortcomings.

It was not always so; this great island race at first viewed the motor car with the very gravest suspicions because it threatened a far older friendship — that of man and horse. Let's be honest: in the 1980s the car is not always viewed with total enthusiasm; in the 1890s and 1900s, it was generally regarded with undisguised hostility.

I am proud to be able to boast that my father was one of those who helped the motor car win a place in society. He championed the cause of motoring in Parliament, becoming the first MP to drive a car into Palace Yard, Westminster, thereby risking the grave displeasure of some and the disapproval of many. Perhaps more importantly, one summer's day in 1899, John Scott-Montagu took Edward, Prince of Wales, for a spin in his Daimler along the roads of the New Forest, sparking a royal enthusiasm for motoring which continues even now.

John Scott-Montagu MP was also the founder and editor of *The Car Illustrated*, one of the world's first car magazines. In its pages he was able to forecast such developments as motorways, by-passes, overhead roads, even the road that we now know as the M25 London Orbital Motorway. He was one of those early enthusiasts who helped the car develop, contributing to the formation of a great industry.

But it took a lot of doing. The car has been reviled, its drivers jeered at, sneered at,

◀My father and the Prince of Wales, later King Edward VII, after their famous spin in 1899 along the roads of the New Forest, a journey which converted the future king to motoring. The two ladies whom he had chaffed throughout the journey had evidently disappeared indoors to repair the ravages of the trip!

prosecuted, taxed and even imprisoned. So how did it start, why was there all the fuss, and how did it develop?

From the beginning of time, man (and woman) has needed and wanted to get around. For millions of years, all he could do was stand up and walk. It meant hard graft on the legs, and blisters and calluses on the feet. And travel was dangerous too; no roads, only paths, mainly through woods, and thickets full of potentially-hostile tribes.

No wonder the early Briton blessed the inventor of the wheel! This gave him the chance to build a cart and drag his family and his belongings around with him — life jumped one step forward. And then, another brainwave! Instead of dragging the cart around, why not get someone else to do it for you! Yoke the cart to one of those nice animals man was just starting to domesticate, and get the ox or horse to do the work instead.

And that was just how it was done in Britain (and indeed elsewhere in the world) for hundreds and hundreds of years. Man and woman, provided they had the wherewithal, could travel in style and even comfort. If you didn't have the wherewithal, you just went on walking, no doubt consumed with envy for those who went by cart or carriage. That irritation exists even now; think of the days when you don't have the use of a car, and how you envy those who do!

Change was slow to come about; new developments were mistrusted. That same reluctance to accept progress in the nineteenth century — not to mention the force of opinion of the railway lobby — led to the establishment of a law obliging the carrying of a red flag ahead of every motor car.

The early Briton discovered that the lighter the construction of his cart, the quicker the ox or horse could tow. He also realised that horses could trot considerably faster than oxen and then worked out that two horses were better than one, and four horses better still — always provided you could control them. The quest for power, speed and handling thus began many thousands of years ago!

Queen Boadicea found that she and her followers could cause all sorts of trouble to the occupying Romans with their chariots; they could rush up to an isolated guardpost, put it out of action

GAMAGE'S of HOLBORN
THE WORLD'S PREMIER MOTOR OUTFITTERS.

OUR BECOMING MOTOR HEAD=GEAR

has received the approval of the *élite* of the Motoring World, whilst our prices are exceedingly moderate. . .

The "Gamage" VOITURETTE.

With Genuine 6 h.p. De Dion Motor **£170** (3 Speeds and Reverse) with TONNEAU.
With 2 Bucket or Phaeton Seats, **150 Guineas.** (Hood £15 extra.)
With 2 Speeds and Reverse, **125 Guineas.**

☞ *WE ARE EXHIBITING AT THE CRYSTAL PALACE.* **Stands 261-262.** ☜

MOTOR CATALOGUE POST FREE.

A. W. GAMAGE, Ltd., HOLBORN, LONDON, E.C.

In the 1980s a lady motor industry executive caused uproar when she suggested that one day Marks and Spencer might sell motor cars. Gamage's were doing it back at the turn of the century! They also made use of the fair sex to sell their cars, something the motor industry has done ever since. The lady on the Gamage's Voiturette looks suitably alarmed, as well she might, as her chauffeur has stopped looking at the road in an effort to select the next gear!

11

Here he is, the infamous man with the red flag marching along, arm raised, while the new motorists hurtle in his wake at four miles an hour. It was the ending of this law which gave motoring a chance to flourish.

with remarkable savagery, and be well away by the time the Roman reinforcements panted up on foot.

Of course, one didn't need a cart or chariot at all. For speed and mobility, hop on to the back of a horse. The family out for a drive in the original horse and cart must have cursed when the sporty horseman spurred-by, leaving them trailing in his wake.

Travelling was a very male business. Women could ride of course — Queen Elizabeth I was a noted horsewoman — but even she took to the carriage for her regal duties. When motoring began, men took the lead, as they did in virtually every other walk of life. Women couldn't vote, couldn't sit in Parliament, couldn't be trusted: *ergo*, they usually didn't drive. All they were encouraged to do was dress in heavy furs, protect their elaborate hair-dos with huge hats and veils and cling on. It was a considerable time before large numbers of women felt the urge to sit behind the wheel, and even today, more men drive than women. There were, of course, notable exceptions to the rule during the pioneering days of the motor car. Honourable mention should be made, for example, of Bertha Benz who drove 112 miles with her two young sons in 1888. This was much further than her husband, the car builder Karl Benz, had yet driven.

The first carts and carriages were quite uncomfortable. It was centuries before matters like suspension were considered, and though the Romans did their best with the roads they built, the collapse of the Roman Empire resulted in nearly one-and-a-half millenia of rutted, bumpy, burglar-and-bandit-ridden tracks. Carriages frequently used long lengths of leather to provide some sort of respite from the potholes, but it cannot have helped very much.

Then came the Industrial Revolution. Metal was used as never before, and James Watt and Richard Trevithick showed what might be done with steam. It worked magnificently with the railway; the iron horse suddenly provided mobility for the masses, travelling up to 100 miles in one day, or even more! But steam was never allowed to work properly on the roads, even though excellent steam-powered road carriages were designed, built and put into service. Why? Well, the railways got there first and represented a considerable threat to the established coaching companies, and in the end they were to do for them altogether. But when the steam carriage was tried for some years, those same companies dampened the project — especially when some of the carriages blew up en route.

Thus it was that Britain turned its back on the roads and went by rail instead. The railways hit Britain in the 1820s — it was to be another 70 years before the motor car was even given the chance to prove itself in these islands. The same combination of ignorance, vested interest and prejudice which allowed the steam-powered road carriage to develop and then killed it off, opposed the car. A series of narrow-minded Acts of Parliament were brought in to restrain 'Road Locomotives'. There was little point British inventors working towards building a motor car which could not be used. Thus it was that two Germans invented the motor car — without those same silly laws, it might well have been a Briton!

It must be remembered, however, that when Karl Benz and Gottlieb Daimler did invent the car, those same Acts of Parliament still applied in Britain. It was to be ten years from the invention of the first car in 1886 to the first 'Emancipation Run', the London to Brighton run of 1896. Herr Daimler himself took part in that run; by then a British Daimler company had been established, and the car was on its way. But that ten years and the ten years that followed remained years of uncertainty.

It was only through the efforts of some great pioneers, allied to royal interest and then royal patronage, that the laws and then the prejudice were slowly dismantled, and the motor car allowed to develop in Britain. It had a very uneasy childhood; one turn-of-the-century MP even went so far as to suggest that motorists should be flogged for disturbing the peace and tranquility of the countryside. My father, also an MP, naturally disagreed. Why then this hatred of the innocent little motor car? The answer is simple — the car didn't have four legs! It was felt that anything which threatened the horse was to be distrusted. The railways provided a good enough way to get about, and indeed many Englishmen made fine fortunes out of railway shares, but this motor car business? The English were not too sure — why should it replace their beautiful gallant friend, the horse? The horse had been good enough for the Greys at Waterloo and good enough for the 'Gallant Six Hundred' during the Charge of the Light Brigade during the Crimea. Even young Lieutenant Churchill of the Fourth Hussars had found the horse a boon when he charged with the British cavalry at the Battle of Omdurman. The horse was founded in British heroic tradition.

And then worse was to come. These motor cars were German, or even French. At any rate, they were certainly foreign. This, remember, was the end of the nineteenth century when the Royal Navy enforced the Pax Britannica at sea and when half a score of invincible battalions were sufficient for Britain — Great Britain — to hold the peace of Europe in her hands.

In addition, motor cars were dangerous. Instead of the friendly horse, or the nice 'chuff-chuff' of the railway engine, one trusted one's life to a machine which was propelled forward as a result of successive explosions in a small box beneath one's feet — it required nerve. When the first British motorists were killed in a crash in Harrow in 1899, there were many who clucked their tongues and moralised on the dangers of this motoring business, conveniently forgetting the hundreds who died each year in accidents with horses.

Nevertheless, despite all the outcry the motor car survived. Those early motorists, clad in heavy fur-lined coats, and sporting goggles which would have done justice to any Phantom of the Opera, probably had no idea of the effects they would have on our twentieth-century world. The motor car has changed all our lives; friends and families now see one another with a frequency which would have amazed our forebears. Journeys, which in the past would have been inconceivable, are now accomplished with comfort, safety and speed.

Motoring is still fun, despite the restrictions and punitive legislation that continues to be heaped on the motorist. Every year, thousands of would-be drivers reach their seventeenth birthday and rush

excitedly towards L-plates, driving schools and the joy of driving and the freedom it gives.

The car has provided employment for hundreds of thousands of people. Even now, in Britain, the motor industry is collectively our biggest employer. It provides jobs and it also creates millions of pounds of taxation which enable us to contribute to the education and welfare services we demand.

Since the early 1890s, Britain has had a strong and steadily-increasing love affair with the motor car. That affair has taken the British all over the world; motor racing, rallying, record-breaking, and just plain travelling. It has made them world champions and speed kings. We may not have invented the car, but having overcome the initial opposition, the British took the car to their hearts and British inventions, such as disc brakes, have continually helped to improve it.

A sobering reminder that for all its new joys, motoring could be a very dangerous undertaking. This was the scene after Britain's first fatal car accident: a Daimler crashed in Harrow, 1899, killing Mr Edwin Sewell and Major Ritchie.

▶The cartoons speak for themselves, but look at the jokes below. Are these the beginning of the 'women driver' jokes?

MOTORING PERSIFLAGE.

THE MANY KINDS OF SPORT WHICH MOTORING INCLUDES.

RIDING

BOXING

GYMNASTICS

TUG OF WAR

SWIMMING

How it Happened.—Bleeker : " Yes, poor Jones lost control of his motor-car."

Baxter : " Heavens ! How did it happen ?"

Bleeker : " Why he foolishly taught his wife how to run it."

The Worst.—" Poor man !" she said, stooping over the victim who had just been dragged out from under her motor-car, " have you a wife ?"

" No," he groaned, " this is the worst thing that ever happened to me."

◀Like father, like son. The chauffeur was a necessity for most pioneer car owners. He had to ensure the car was ready for all weathers, and be proficient in tackling the dirty mechanical jobs. Many chauffeurs were coachmen who converted to the new machines. The chauffeur of this Star obviously had a son ready to step into his boots.

The first motor cars came to Britain from Germany. Gottlieb Daimler and Karl Benz, working no more than 60 miles apart in the Neckar Valley in south-western Germany, each developed his own motor car in 1886. Today, the two companies they founded, are united as Daimler-Benz, the makers of Mercedes Benz buses, trucks, vans and cars. When the two companies both started selling cars in Britain, they were in strict competition. It was not until after the First World War that they merged. Yet in their own lifetimes Daimler and Benz were rivals. They never even met.

However, Daimler and Benz could never have made their cars without the work of another German, Nikolaus Otto. He it was who established the principle of the internal combustion engine, with its classic four-stroke cycle. Without Otto there would not have been an engine, and without an engine there would never have been a car, at least not of the sort we understand.

The early cars were quite remarkable machines. The first Daimler was very much a horseless carriage, complete to the point where the shafts of the harness had been cut off. In place of the horses, an engine was fitted beneath the carriage, driving the rear wheels. The engine was ignited not by spark-plugs, but by 'hot-tube' ignition. A piece of sealed metal tube was run into the engine cylinder and heated to red hot from the outside. The petrol/air mixture entered the cylinder and hit the hot metal, promptly exploding, and forcing the engine piston down. (Promptly that is,

▶This pioneer deserves more than any other to have the title 'father of the British motor industry'. Frederick R. Simms helped bring car manufacturing into Britain through his connection with Daimler in Germany. Here he is testing his armoured reconnaisance quadricycle in Richmond Park in 1899.

GOGGLES.

Superior Rubber Goggles, 1 pair spare glasses supplied with each.
XG70   Best London made. Only the best quality Rubber used Per pair **2/2.** Per doz. pair **24/-**
XG71   Second Quality, French make. Per pair **1/10** Per doz. pair **19/-**
XG72   Rubber Goggles with unbreakable glasses. Per pair **3/-** Per doz. **33/-**

XG73   The "Kerry" Special. The most comfortable goggle made. Long D shaped Nickel frame, with patent swing bar to hold glasses, edged silk, velvet and chenille or rubber, Nickel spring nose bridge, long D shaped bent glasses, easily removed Per pair **4/-** Per doz. **22/-**

XG74   Well finished Nickel Capsules, comfortable fittings, edged silk, velvet and chenille, elastic nose piece, pear shaped glasses. A cheap and neat goggle. … per pair **1 6**

XG77   Glasses in Aluminium Frames chamois mounts, flexible, unlined, satin bound, ventilated … per pair **2 9**

XG76   Nickel Rim, with transparent horn sides, edged chenille, best bent oval glasses … per pair **3 4**

XG75   The "Le Grand" Reflex Goggles for forward and rearward vision. Per pair **10/-**

XG78   Mica Masks, with chenille edges and elastic bands … each **2 8**

XG81   Glasses edged with Aluminium Silk, elastic nose bridge, bound chenille, best quality elastic band with clips … per pair **3 -**

XG79   Glasses in Aluminium Frames, chamois mounts, elastic bands, flexible, white kid lined, ventilated, with nose cover, best finish   per pair **3 8.**

XG80   Mica Eye Shields, superfine quality, unique shape, chenille bound, elastic bands … each **4 2**

XG85   Light Wire Frame, shaped to face, Silk covered, edged chenille, leather nose piece, pear shaped glasses in oval rims … per pair **3 6**

XG82   Leather Cloth, unlined, spring clips to hold glasses. Cheap line but good … … per pair **3 -**
XG83   Four D Glass Goggles in Folding frame, leather mask lined white kid bound plush, glasses interchangeable, ventilated, elastic bands, patent swing bar to hold glass   per pair **4 -**

XG84 Glasses, very large, metal frames folding, leather, chenille bound, ventilated, elastic bands … per pair **3 4**

XG86   The New Rain and Sun Shield Goggles. Type 197. Fitted with Collapsible Shield over Glasses. Per pair … … **11**

Many and varied were the types of goggles the early motorist could buy and wear. They were highly necessary, because the grit and dust of the roads could cause damage to the eyes. The most luxurious here is Le Grand Reflex model — priced at 10/- for forward and rearward vision!

MOTOR ✄ ✄ KERRY ✄ SPECIALITIES

HORNS.

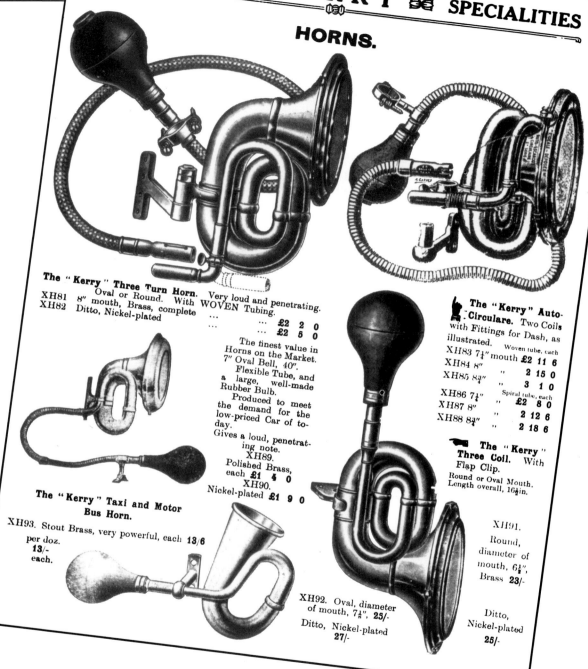

The "Kerry" Three Turn Horn. Very loud and penetrating. With WOVEN Tubing.

XH81 Oval or Round. 8" mouth, Brass, complete **£2 2 0**
XH82 Ditto, Nickel-plated **£2 5 0**

The finest value in Horns on the Market. 7" Oval Bell, 40". Flexible Tube, and a large, well-made Rubber Bulb. Produced to meet the demand for the low-priced Car of to-day. Gives a loud, penetrating note.

XH89. Polished Brass, each **£1 4 0**
XH90. Nickel-plated **£1 9 0**

☞ **The "Kerry" Auto-Circulare.** Two Coils with Fittings for Dash, as illustrated.

Woven tube, each
XH83 7¼" mouth **£2 11 6**
XH84 8" " **2 15 0**
XH85 8¾" " **3 1 0**

Spiral tube, each
XH86 7¼" " **£2 8 0**
XH87 8" " **2 12 6**
XH88 8¾" " **2 18 6**

The "Kerry" Three Coil. With Flap Clip. Round or Oval Mouth. Length overall, 16½in.

XH91. Round, diameter of mouth, 6½", Brass **23/-**

Ditto, Nickel-plated **25/-**

The "Kerry" Taxi and Motor Bus Horn.

XH93. Stout Brass, very powerful, each **13/6** per doz. **13/-** each.

XH92. Oval, diameter of mouth, 7⅛", **25/-**
Ditto, Nickel-plated **27/-**

Some early car horns would not have looked out of place mounted as sirens aboard a battleship: Manufacturers were keen to advise that the horns had a loud and penetrating note, making pioneers even more unpopular with passers-by and residents!

provided the hot tube was hot enough.) And it was earlier steam cars which gave us the term 'chauffeur', literally meaning the stoker or fireman of a steam engine.

Curiously, Daimler himself had a considerable connection with Britain. He came here as a student in the 1860s, and worked in engineering firms in Leeds and Coventry, later the home of the British Daimler company. He apparently liked the British, and the British respected his technical and engineering ability, and undoubted ambition.

Daimler and his rival Benz's cars soon attracted a good deal of attention, not all of it friendly. The *Mannheimer Zeitung* called the Benz car, 'ridiculous and indecent'; the *Cannstatter Zeitung* dubbed the Daimler, 'repugnant and diabolical'. Similar language was used when the car came to Britain.

Several men can claim the credit for promoting the motor car: H.J. Lawson, an entrepreneur who ended up in jail; Sir David Salomons, Mayor of Tunbridge Wells, who organised Britain's first-ever Motor Show in 1895, and the astonishingly energetic Frederick R. Simms. Simms was a remarkable man; he had already made and patented a machine for automatically dispensing railway tickets, designed an aerial ropeway system, and he would go on to design and demonstrate his military quadricycle. In due course he would set up the main trade association for the British motor industry, the Society of Motor Manufacturers and Traders, which still exists today.

Simms tried to bring Daimler engines in to Britain but kept running up against those who feared the machines would blow up. He could not import a car and when he tried to demonstrate the engine-driving machinery at a German Exhibition at Earl's Court, he was banned. The authorities even refused to let him use the engine in a boat on the Serpentine. The British establishment were

The man holding the boat-like tiller is Herbert Austin, who later founded the Austin company. Here he is on the 1899 Wolseley which he drove in the One Thousand Mile Trial of 1900 when he was chief designer and engineer for Wolesely.

clearly unwilling to allow a small German explosive device to be demonstrated — it might, after all, alarm the horses, to say nothing of the general public.

But there were few horses to be alarmed on the River Thames, and eventually in 1891, Simms was able to show the new Daimler engine in use, running up and down off Charing Cross pier. Four years later, Simms and his friends formed *The Autocar,* the first car magazine in Britain, and in June that year, defying the law, they imported a car — a Panhard & Levassor, fitted with a Daimler engine — and drove it to Windsor. The same car was used that October as one of the four entrants in Britain's first Motor Show. Sir David Salomons made the arrangements, included his own Peugeot car, and set out to amaze the public.

By now the ball was rolling. A company had been formed to make and sell Daimler cars under licence in Britain, known as the Daimler Motor Company of Coventry. Moves were afoot to force the repeal of the punitive restrictions which had kept cars off the road. There was another Motor Show, on a much grander scale, this time in London. And then, in November 1896, came a new Act of Parliament.

This was The Light (Road) Locomotives Act. It raised the speed limit to no less than 12 miles per hour and scrapped the requirement for the man to walk in front of the car. It was the start of a social revolution. To celebrate, on 14 November 1896, 35 vehicles set out from Northumberland Avenue in London to drive to Brighton. The London to Brighton run is still held today, of course, always on the first Sunday in November. Though restricted to cars built before 1905, it now attracts almost 400 entries a year.

My father was one of the supporters of The Light (Road) Locomotives Act. He had his first ride on a motor car (early motorists always travelled on rather than in a car) the year after the first Emancipation Run, and promptly decided to buy a car of his own.

Naturally, John Scott-Montagu bought a British-built Daimler. Daimlers were the dominant marque in Britain, and everyone associated with the fledgling industry seemed to own one. So the first Daimler came to Beaulieu, to the delight of

John's family and the amusement, perhaps bemusement, of the village. It was a six horsepower Daimler wagonette with hot-tube ignition, tiller steering and chain drive. A big tank at the back was filled with water which slowly trickled through the engine to cool it down. When the tank was empty, fresh supplies of water had to be found before the motoring could continue. My father recalled, years later, that every bump would cause the tiller to be almost wrenched out of his hand, the springing was 'primitive' and the bumping 'severe'. He was indeed an intrepid young motorist!

Whatever his friends and neighbours may have felt, John Scott-Montagu leapt into motoring with an extraordinary enthusiasm. He joined Frederick Simms' Automobile Club of Great Britain and Ireland, bought a second, much more powerful Daimler, and proceeded to take on the establishment from within.

Parliament might have passed The Light (Road) Locomotives Act sooner, but there was still great prejudice against the car, not least from within the House itself. Scott-Montagu decided on a daring PR coup; he ventured to drive his car into Palace Yard, Westminster, at the heart of the Mother of Parliaments. He was turned back by the police sergeant on duty who told him, 'them things is excluded by the Order of the Speaker because we never know when it might set the building on fire'! John appealed for the ancient right of MPs for access, but the confrontation with authority had caught the attention of the Press, and they gave the affair full coverage. It may seem little enough now, but it was hot news then.

During the Recess that summer, my father achieved his greatest coup: Edward, Prince of Wales, was thought to be favourable to the idea of motoring. He had travelled a short distance on several cars, once at the Motor Show at the Imperial Institute in London, once in an excursion from Warwick Castle. In August 1899, the Prince was staying at Highcliffe Castle, near Christchurch, in the New Forest. John Scott-Montagu was bidden to lunch and after the meal he dared to suggest a motor drive to the King-to-be. A sportsman and gentleman, Bertie agreed. Two lady members of the lunch party were installed in the back seats, the Prince sat down in front, my father squeezed in beside him, and off they drove.

They evidently had great fun, with the Prince in good humour. He chaffed the ladies incessantly, teased my father, and enjoyed himself enormously, cigar in hand. In later years, John Scott-Montagu recalled that the Prince evidently realised the changes cars would make to the land he would shortly rule as King-Emperor.

A few weeks later, my father was asked to take his car to the Prince's London residence, Marlborough House. Here it was examined by officials, and shortly afterwards the order for the first royal Daimler was placed. Edward, Prince of Wales, may not have realised it — though I suspect very much that he did — but by buying the first royal car he became the unofficial Patron of motoring in Britain and society started to accept it.

Once royalty in this great country supports an idea, it tends to develop in the minds of others. It was not only Daimler who were making and selling cars; old-established British firms like Wolseley, who had made sheep-shearing machines, and Humber, who made bicycles, were thinking about cars too.

In 1900, my father took part in the first One Thousand Mile Trial in Britain. It was organised by the Automobile Club, and among the other entrants who set out from London on St George's Day were Herbert Austin on a Wolseley, the Hon. C.S. Rolls driving a Panhard and Selwyn F. Edge aboard a Napier. All three would become famous in their lifetimes. The idea of the Trial was to prove the worth and reliability of the motor car. The Prince of Wales might have bought one, daring young bloods-around-town and youthful MPs might own them, but surely these cars were not to be taken seriously. That was the view of many, reinforced by coachmen and stable-boys, anxious to maintain the status quo and their livelihoods.

The Trial went right round the country, giving public exhibitions wherever and whenever it could find a crowd. The cars travelled to Bristol, Birmingham, and Manchester, through the Lake District to Carlisle and up to Edinburgh. Then southwards to Newcastle-upon-Tyne, Leeds, Sheffield and Nottingham, and home to London. They attracted civic dignitaries, nobility and gentry, and the attention of the police! The speed limit was still 12 miles per hour, and constables gathered at regular intervals to try and catch those who broke it.

65 cars set off of which 35 completed the full distance. It was tough going; hill-climbs, including one run up Shap Fell (over 1,300 feet above sea level) and nowadays the summit of the M6. The roads were dreadful, with mud and dust plaguing the contestants, and potholes wreaking havoc with wheels and suspension. But it achieved what it set out to do. After the One Thousand Mile Trial, no-one could dismiss the car as a mere plaything.

The ten years between 1896 and 1906 saw a complete revolution in motoring and in car design. The early cars were quite simply horseless carriages, but around the turn of the century, cars suddenly began to get lower and lower, and the standard layout of the motor car began to be adopted. The engine went at the front, under a bonnet, with the gearbox behind. Then came the driver and passengers, sitting behind the engine and gearbox and ahead of the rear axle. Compare the 1896 Daimler in which Herr Daimler himself travelled on the original London to Brighton Run with the Star Racer which took part in the Gordon Bennett trials. The transformation from horseless carriage to motor car was already complete.

My father decided not long after the One Thousand Mile Trial to try his hand at publishing. He was already a key man in the motoring world, with access to royalty and to Parliament, now as Editor and Publisher of *The Car Illustrated* he

▶Proof of the need for the goggles and the protective clothing for the elimination trials for the 1905 Gordon Bennett Race. There is no weather protection on board the Star Racer ... and the two policemen in the background are about to be enveloped in that cloud of dust. The photographing of early racing was very difficult: there was no fast film and shutter speeds to capture the scene, and the pioneer Grand Prix cameramen deserve praise for their efforts.

This, at an initial glance, could be a sketch of the M25 junction with the M23. It was drawn by my father as long ago as 1911, described then as 'an artist's dream of what the Road Board may accomplish'. Although he was a member of that Board they did not accomplish it.

could take the campaign to the public. He was helped by Alfred Harmsworth, the owner of the *Daily Mail* and the future Lord Northcliffe, who let the MP work for him for a while as a reporter. The first edition of *The Car Illustrated* was published at the end of May 1902, with a front-cover picture of King Edward VII at the wheel of a giant 24 horsepower Daimler.

The Car Illustrated became a legend in motoring journalism, predicting the London Orbital Motorway 80 years or so before it was completed, and publishing in 1911 a remarkably accurate drawing of how the M25 would look. Planners and politicians take their time: the M25 was completed in 1986 and the M1 in the Sixties, though my father argued for them before the First World War, a full seven decades earlier!

Three other great enthusiasts must be honoured at this point: Henry Royce and the Hon. C.S. Rolls, and Selwyn Francis Edge. Rolls and Royce have their place in history, and deservedly so, but less is remembered nowadays about S.F. Edge. He, more than anyone else, brought business methods and sales techniques to the British motor industry. His own firm, S.F. Edge & Company, sold the Napier car, and he was not afraid to put the product to the test himself. A big, brash and bouncy Australian, Edge was as tough as they come. He took part in a Napier in the One Thousand Mile Trial, and then drove another to victory in the Gordon Bennett Cup race in 1902. The Gordon Bennett races were the Grand Prix and Monte-Carlo rallies of their day, rolled into one. Speed, endurance and reliability were needed concurrently. That victory did much to sell the Napier as a sporting car, but it was in 1907 that Edge had his very finest hour. In that year, the world's first purpose-built motor racing circuit was completed, at Brooklands in Surrey. Today, Brooklands is a sad place, with most of its former

Selwyn Francis Edge on the Napier at Brooklands where in 1907 he set up the 24-hour record at over 60 miles an hour. The man in the winding sheet beside him is the riding mechanic. Mr Edge was a tough man: so was his mechanic who experienced all the danger and none of the fame.

glory gone, though the Brooklands Museum does sterling work to recapture what remains. In 1907 it was a very exciting place indeed. The brainchild of another Edwardian enthusiast, Hugh Locke-King, Brooklands was built on his estate. 200,000 tons of cement were used to make a grand oval circuit, distinguished by huge banked corners. The purpose of the circuit was unclear to some, who believe Mr Locke-King wanted the track to be used for test purposes by car manufacturers. But in any event, Brooklands, close to the railway lines to London, and not far from the A3, became ideal for motor sport.

Edge planned to make a grand gesture and announced glibly that he would take his new Napier around the track for no less than 24 hours at an average speed of 60 miles per hour. The Press were astonished, the public amazed, and medical experts horrified. Napier's own engineers were terrified too; they did not know how the car would perform when asked to go at full speed for 24 hours. In fact they were forced to make frantic improvements to the cooling system of the great car to enable it to achieve the time and speed demanded. But it worked! With the track lit by huge flaming braziers set at regular intervals, Edge and the Napier thundered through the night, his racing mechanic huddled by his side, using the complicated lubricating system before him on the dashboard to maintain a steady flow of oil to parts of the machinery likely to overheat.

Edge beat his own target, bringing the Napier through the 24 hours at a speed of over 65 miles per hour! Sales of the Napier were boosted and it won a reputation for record-breaking which remained for the next three, even four, decades if cars with Napier aero-engines are included in the reckoning. Edge made a sensational name for himself, as legendary then as any Stirling Moss or Jackie Stewart. And the motor car passed another huge milestone. In addition, the notion of motor racing and motor sport 'improving the breed' was put firmly into the engineers' and sales managers' heads. In future, British firms would turn to motor sport to test their theories, and win sales for their products.

For a car race track Brooklands was run at first on somewhat unusual lines; there was no tradition of motor sport, so it had to be invented, or at least borrowed. The gentlemen who got together to set up motor racing at Brooklands, under the title of the Brooklands Automobile Racing Club knew exactly where to turn to borrow that tradition. Their fathers and grandfathers, and indeed they themselves, were great supporters of the turf, and so motor racing acquired most of its early manners from horse racing! And remember: a decade or so earlier the motor car was viewed as a deadly threat to man's oldest friend. In its pragmatic manner, the British establishment had looked at the motor car and decided to put up with it, and blend it within its own traditions.

In the very first races, the drivers all wore different-coloured shirts, just as jockeys wear the different colours or 'silks' of their owners. That custom lasted no more than a few months, because motor racing at speeds over 60 miles per hour made the colours difficult to identify, and so the practice spread to the cars themselves.

One may wonder why the British race in green. There are a lot of theories on this habit, but it relates to those early motor races held before Brooklands was built. Previously, motor racing took place on public roads, and a pretty dangerous business it was. My father had been the first Englishman to appear in a British made car in one of the very early road races, racing alongside the Hon. C.S. Rolls in the 1899 Paris-Ostend race. The two were in different classes but they were both racing for Britain. There were crashes and spills; John Scott-Montagu suffered breakdowns and punctures but was third in his class. Rolls did well in his Panhard car, winning second place overall, but the event gave my father another enthusiasm, that for motor sport.

The 1902 Gordon Bennett race, from Paris to Innsbruck, was won by S.F. Edge. My father and his friends at the Automobile Club knew that under the rules of the event, the country which held the trophy had the right to stage the following year's race, and that was clearly impossible under current British legislation. British law laid down that cars could not exceed a speed of 12 miles per hour, and motorists who did were liable to prosecution. The months went by, and no solution was found. The race had to be held in Britain and yet could not be. It would be a valuable boost to the fledgling British motor industry, and yet it looked likely that the British would have to go red-faced to the Trophy committee and admit they could not stage the event. At which point the Irish Question entered the scene. It had dominated British domestic politics for years, but this time it was not a problem but a solution; a group of Irishmen suggested that the race be held not in Britain, but in Ireland. My father, journalist, Member of Parliament, motorist and motor racer, and vice-chairman of the Automobile Club of Great Britain and Ireland, saw a last-minute way out. He moved The Light Locomotives (Ireland) Bill, which

▶Early pioneers had to wrap up well to stay warm when on their motor cars. There was little or no weather protection, and the exposed position could chill a man to the marrow. Hence the motoring coat, lined with fur, in which the early driver sought some shelter from the elements.

"KERRY" WEAR FOR MOTORISTS.

Wonderful Value in
FUR LINED COATS.

IRISH FRIEZE, FUR LINED.

These Ulsters are supplied in a variety of patterns of Irish Frieze Cloths, **lined with warm Fur.** A most comfortable and cosy garment for motoring, and wonderful value.

		Each.
No. MC500	Frieze, Lined Hamster	£5 17 9
No. MC501	,, ,, Electric Rabbit	£6 15 0
No. MC502	,, ,, Marmot (whole skins)	£9 9 0
No. MC503	,, ,, Marmot (pieced skins)	£6 0 0
No. MC504	,, ,, Dyed Wallaby	£9 0 0
No. MC505	,, ,, Musquash	£12 0 0

BLACK BEAVER, FUR LINED with FUR COLLARS.

		Each.
No. MC510	Beaver, lined black electric rabbit with electric collar	£15 0 0
No. MC511	Beaver, lined Marmot with nutria Beaver collar	£15 0 0
No. MC512	Beaver, lined rabbit with Persian Lamb collar	£15 0 0
No. MC513	Beaver, lined Musquash with Persian Lamb **long roll collar**	£21 0 0

		Each.
No. MC506	West of England Cloth, lined Musquash	£15 0 0
No. MC507	Irish Cheviot, lined Musquash	£12 0 0

City of Nottingham and County of the same City.

MOTOR CAR ACT, 1903.

Licence No. 9737 to Drive a Motor Car.

Albert Edward Dakin
of 26 Parkinson Street, Station St.
is hereby licensed to drive a MOTOR CAR for the period of **Twelve Months** from the
13th day of May 1915 until the 12th
day of May 1916 inclusive. W. J. Board
M.S. Town Clerk.

ENDORSEMENTS.

At Bow Street Police Court London
Date of Conviction:- 30th June 1906
Offence:- Emitting visible vapour in a Royal
Park.
Sentence:- Fined £4 & 2/- costs

At Bow Street Police Court London
Date of Conviction:- 6th May 1907
Offence:- Emitting visible vapour in a Royal
Park.
Sentence:- Fined £3 & 2/- costs

G. Kirkwood R.a

◀The most famous motorist of the Edwardian era, the Hon. Charles Stuart Rolls, at the wheel of a Rolls-Royce shortly before his death in 1910. Rolls was killed flying: as an aviation pioneer, he was the first man to fly from England to France and back again. My father and Rolls raced together in France before the turn of the century.

◀(*Inset*) Unsociable Mr Albert Edward Dakin discharged visible vapour in a Royal Park not once but twice, and was duly convicted for it. The fines of £4 and £3 were severe.

would provide for the closure of certain roads in Ireland and the suspension of the speed limit on those roads for the duration of the race.

With one or two initial hiccups, the Bill was passed through the Commons and the Lords. But it then came up against quite surprising opposition — the King was worried and concerned. He knew the dangers, and the deaths and injuries of the Paris-Madrid race of 1903 worried him deeply. However, he received reassurances as to the safety precautions that would be taken, and gave the Royal Assent. The 1903 Gordon Bennett race went ahead, with the British racing in green, out of deference, it is said, to the Irish shamrock. For the record, the race was won by a German Mercedes, with the French team picking up the new Montagu Trophy for the best team placing. The first car to wear the green — which has been worn ever since — was the 45-horsepower Napier which came in fifth, driven by Charles Jarrott. Always recognised as Britain's oldest racing car it was rescued from the United States in 1987 with assistance from the National Heritage Memorial Fund and a public appeal. It is now on display at the National Motor Museum.

While all these life-and-death motor races and record-breaking feats were happening, there was much agitation to do away with the old 12 miles per hour speed limit. It was highly restrictive, not only to drivers, but also to manufacturers, and the British were clearly suffering. After considerable time and work, what began life as the Scott-Montagu Bill, The Motor Vehicles Registration Bill, became the Government's own Motor Car Act. On 1 January 1904 it raised the speed limit to 20 miles per hour and provided for the

registration of vehicles, the display of number plates and the requirement for drivers and cars to obtain a licence. The new law was not much of an advance on the old, to modern eyes, yet it was part of the many moves bringing motoring within the British way of life. Policemen still lay in wait for unwary motorists, timing them over sections of road and dragging them off to court — indeed the new Automobile Association was set up in 1905 to help drivers combat the police threat. But from this point, motoring was firmly established as part of British heritage.

While my father was helping enact legislation, and Edge was planning his record-breaking, a meeting took place which was vital to the whole future of the British motor industry and which would give it its proudest name. Claude Edmunds, one of the founders of the Automobile Club, brought together the engineer Henry Royce, and the Hon. C.S. Rolls. Rolls was already well-known; like my father he was part of the aristocracy and moved in high society, when he was not selling Panhard cars from his showrooms in Fulham. He it was who had taken the future Queen Mary for her first drive back in 1900 and who thought nothing of travelling hundreds of miles across country, often having to sleep under his car, to visit the great houses of his friends, and extol the virtues of the car.

Royce was a brilliant, meticulous engineer, who had fought his way up from poverty to own his own electrical engineering firm. He wanted to make cars and Rolls knew how to sell them. They met in Manchester and the rest is history. Rolls was killed in a plane crash in 1910, Royce worked himself almost to death building cars and aero-engines, but the company they set up established the reputation of British automotive excellence

▶The world's most famous motoring pin-up, and the lady who inspired her. On the left, the Spirit of Ecstacy, the Flying Lady who has graced Rolls-Royces since Edwardian times, and perched on the right, my father's secretary and devoted companion, Eleanor Thornton, who modelled for the sculptor Charles Sykes to create it. My father's RAC and AA badges can also be seen: later he took this car to India with him.

around the world.

They achieved this by one magnificent publicity trick. In 1907, they took the thirteenth model of their new 40/50 horsepower car off the assembly line, painted it silver, and added all sorts of silver-plated accessories and equipment. Claude Johnson, the firm's managing director, with a variety of passengers, including on one occasion my father, set off to drive back and forth between London and Glasgow on a 15,000 mile reliability trial.

The great silver car, remarkable for its silent mode of travel, went back and forth, stopping only for petrol, water, and for tyre changes and punctures. It smashed the old records, and with the consequent publicity in the Press — including special articles in *The Car Illustrated* — the legend of Rolls-Royce for smooth, silent and wholly reliable travel went right around the world. The Royal Family stuck to their Daimlers but the rich and fashionable turned increasingly to the Rolls-Royce. From then until 1925, Rolls-Royce cars were named in deference to that great silver car, proceeding strongly, silently, like a ghost. It became known as the Silver Ghost, and is in Rolls-Royce Motors' ownership today.

My father became an immense enthusiast for Rolls-Royce and ordered his own car. But he had a hand, too, in another Rolls-Royce tradition, and one still famous today. Around 1910 a craze began for putting mascots on the radiators of cars. Many were unsuitable for this purpose and the directors of Rolls-Royce commissioned the sculptor and illustrator Charles Sykes to make a suitable mascot to appear exclusively on Rolls-Royce radiators. Sykes had shot to fame through his work for *The Car Illustrated,* and he took as his model for the project my father's personal assistant and secretary, Eleanor Thornton. Thus it was that 'The Spirit of Ecstasy', the famous Rolls-Royce 'Flying Lady', was modelled on the secretary for a leading car magazine.

By the end of the first decade of the twentieth century, motoring had become an important part of British life. The motor car was still not fully accepted — on one occasion Lady Montagu had to duck when a telephone insulator was thrown at her car — and the Law was still less than convinced about the morals and the wisdom of drivers. But the car had survived its infancy.

Coachmen and stable-lads had adapted to the car, becoming chauffeurs and assistants in the big motor-houses that had been built alongside stately homes. Where a son might have followed his father and become a coachman, now he looked forward to joining him as, perhaps, second chauffeur. The real enthusiasts, however, like my father, Rolls, Edge and their friends, preferred to drive themselves. But if the car needed repairing, the chauffeur did the work. When it needed cleaning, he scrubbed and polished and burnished the paintwork.

The Edwardian age was, for motoring, the age of the chauffeur. And he had a lot to do when driving the new big cars like the Rolls-Royce, the Napier, the Lanchester or the Daimler. Ahead of him, a huge steering wheel, huge because there was no power steering and the driver needed to have all the help he could get turning the wheel at low speeds. In the middle of the steering wheel, a variety of controls: levers to adjust the slow running of the engine, to adjust the mixture of petrol and air being passed into the cylinders, to adjust the point at which the spark was generated inside the cylinder to ignite the mixture. The Rolls-Royce could be started 'on the Switch'; move the ignition control lever back and forth between 'Early' and 'Late', and the car would normally fire up. It certainly sometimes saved one getting out and turning the massive engine over on the starting handle! There was a right and a wrong way to do that too. Wrap the hand around the handle, and if the engine backfired, the luckless chauffeur could break his wrist. It was vital to keep the thumb on the same side of the handle as the rest of the fingers! Meters and dials told the chauffeur something of what was going on in the car beneath him, but often it was a matter of listening to the engine beat, worrying over lubrication and petrol pressure, even smelling the air to make sure something was not getting too hot.

On the Silver Ghost, both the handbrake and gearlever were to the right of the driver. The handbrake was not only designed for parking — it was an absolute necessity when trying to slow down at all. In fact, the Rolls-Royce only had

brakes on its back wheels. It was not until the Twenties that the Rolls-Royce acquired four wheel brakes.

One of the big charges against the motor car in the Edwardian era was the dust it created. The early roads had benefited from the pioneering work of Macadam, but even when they were paved according to Macadam's precepts, they

The steering wheel of my father's Rolls-Royce. The beautifully turned controls on the wheel itself controlled mixture, engine speed and ignition timing. Rolls-Royces would start 'on the Switch': waggling the ignition control on the right between 'Early' and 'Late' would induce a spark in one or other of the cylinders, and the great car would start. Note the gear shift and hand brake on the right hand side.

were not designed for the motor car at all. Carriages and other horse-drawn vehicles threw up some dust as they trailed by behind their trotting or straining horses, but the cars threw the dust high up in the air. The dust blanketed everything it touched. Bright green hedges turned grey, windows on houses went opaque and washing was ruined. It was nasty and anti-social. My father set up a Dust Fund through *The Car Illustrated,* and experiments were carried out at Sutton Place in Surrey. The answer was at hand — tar.

The tarring of macadamised roads and the wooden-blocks that paved so many city streets was to revolutionise motoring. It made it safe and far more comfortable to travel, and it made the car far less offensive to other road users and to local inhabitants. It also helped to cut down the number of punctures, which were the bugbear of the early drivers. The tiny stones would cut their way through the tyre covers, aided and abetted by the thousands of horseshoe nails that littered the roadways. The tyre would puncture, the car had to stop, and driver and passengers make repairs. Gradually the tyres grew stronger and more resistant, horses began to disappear from the roads, and the new tarmacadamed streets ended the menace from stones, as well as ending the dust crisis.

The motor car was now regarded in Britain as a pastime, a way of life, for the weathly man. The gentry and the nobility might glide effortlessly by, but the nearest an ordinary man or woman might come to travelling by car was as a chauffeur or a servant, or if he or she took a taxi in the metropolis. When war broke out in August 1914, the situation was changing. The first great Ford plant had been set up in Manchester, at Trafford Park, and was actually producing more cars than any other company in Britain. But it was to take the First World War to bring the notion of car travel, and even car ownership, to the rest of the people.

The gentlemen on the left are the really significant part of this picture ... they are ready to lay down tar on the road to bind the road surface together. It was the tarring of roads that ended the dust nightmare which had caused so much anger amongst non-motorists.

MOTORING AND THE GREAT WAR

It was to be the most terrifying war the world had ever known, called the Great War to distinguish it from all others. It was the hand of a Serbian nationalist, Gavrilo Princip, that started the horror, and a motor car was involved. The Archduke Franz Ferdinand and his wife were being driven through the streets of Sarajevo in an open Gräf und Stift car when Princip fired. They did not stand a chance. The interlocking series of military alliances across Europe meant that war was all but inevitable, mobilisation was ordered, and four years of horror began.

It was called 'war by railway timetable', because once mobilisation began, nothing could stop it, and because for years it had been recognised that the railways were strategically vital for the movement of troops to the war zones. French railway trucks carried the words '8 Chevaux, 40 Hommes' to show their troop or horse-carrying capacity. But if the Grand Armée of France, and the armies of the Kaiser, the King-Emperor and the Tsar of All the Russias went to war by railway, their officers — certainly their senior officers — made sure they took a few cars along with them.

Previous wars had seen horses called up in great numbers from the stables of the nobility and gentry. This time their cars were volunteered or requisitioned as well; motor transport was to prove vital to the conduct of the war whether fought in the mud of the Western Front, in the desert with Lawrence, or even in India. Thousands of men and women were taught to drive — witness the despatch riders, the staff cars, the tanks and the ambulances.

Those same cars which had outraged society at the turn of the century with their noisy din, their dust and their frightening speed were quite suddenly, less than 15 years later, in great demand. The car makers sucked their teeth and looked at their ranges. Chassis were strengthened, springing toned up, and needless luxuries like lined

◀ The armoured Rolls-Royce, advocated by my father and used so effectively by Lawrence in the desert and elsewhere. Note the shutters for the radiator and the machine gun. Years later Vickers — who made the gun — were to take over Rolls-Royce Motors.

My father as Brigadier-General pictured against the background of the Khyber Pass roads he insisted were vital to keep the North-West Frontier secure. The Government took more notice of his demand for roads in India than they did when after the War he campaigned for a London to Birmingham motorway!

hoods and extra lamps and equipment done away with, and the assembly lines began to turn out cars for the Forces.

One of the most popular models was the 25 horsepower Vauxhall, adopted for use by the War Office. It came in handy for all sorts of roles: providing transport for staff officers through the mud of Flanders or taking the King-Emperor past rows and rows of the Royal Scots and other regiments, giving them the royal eye of inspection before they were plunged into the hell of the trenches.

The Vauxhall certainly had the pedigree for such roles. Only a few years before it had swept the board in the famous Prince Henry Trials, a testing car event held at the behest of the Kaiser's brother,

The 'poor bloody infantry' watch the staff officers sweep by in lofty arrogance in their Vauxhall.

Prince Henry of Prussia. As a result, the company had called its top model the Prince Henry Vauxhall, and it sold well. But pity the poor infantry struggling up to the Line, dragging horses and baggage wagons through the mire, while the staff officers drove by.

While Vauxhall, Sunbeam, Crossley and firms like them were providing the wheels of the Western Front, in the desert it was very different. The potential of the car for desert warfare was quite obvious; hard surfaces, swept by the incessant winds, provided the very ground a big

car could use, and the car that fitted the part was the Rolls-Royce. If Edge and Rolls and their friends were the complete British motorists from the age of discovery, then Colonel T.E. Lawrence, Lawrence of Arabia, has to be one of the motorists of the war years. He wrote that a 'Rolls in the desert is beyond rubies', a simple statement of fact that would no doubt have appealed to the desert sheiks whose motley forces he transformed into an effective fighting army.

My father was also involved in the use of the Rolls-Royce as a fighting vehicle. Colonel Lord Montagu was recalled to the Colours along with many other Territorial officers when the war broke out. After a spell in London looking after a group of enthusiasts who had placed themselves and their vehicles at the disposal of the authorities, he sailed for India in command of a Territorial battalion of the Hampshire Regiment. They were going to India to free the regular troops serving there to return to fight in France. Once in India, Lord Montagu was given a post as Inspector of Motor Vehicles on the Indian Army General Staff. It allowed him to confirm the conclusions he already had made; that the car, in armoured guise, was an ideal way of keeping the peace among rebellious tribesmen on the North-West Frontier and anywhere else. He was sent back to London to make urgent representations at the War Office for more motor transport for India, but not before he had laid the groundwork for the first Armoured Motor Unit, consisting of three Rolls-Royce armoured cars. He had also realised the need for aircraft for the far-flung battle line of Empire — aircraft which would, and in time did, patrol the fringes and boundaries of the British Empire and keep trouble at bay.

Converting a Rolls-Royce into an armoured car was an interesting exercise. You needed first of all to strengthen the chassis, and provide twin wheels at the rear for improved traction. Then it was vital to cover up with armour plate all the parts of the car which could be susceptible to a bullet. These naturally enough included the radiator. But how to cover the radiator with plate without it boiling over? The problem was solved by fitting doors, which would prevent anything but a direct hit when open, and which could be drawn shut from within the car when even that became a possibility. Petrol tanks had to be strengthened and protected, a swivelling turret provided over the passenger compartment, and a visor fitted so the driver could see exactly where he was going. It sounds very cumbersome and no doubt to the modern motorist it would be. But to those who were fighting in the desert it was a wonder — faster than a horse or camel, invulnerable to almost any attack, and spitting death and defiance from

the Vickers machine gun mounted in the turret. The British had found a machine more than suitable to wage war.

Not all Rolls-Royces were armoured; many were used for the transport of generals. General Sir John French had his Rolls-Royce delivered at the very outset of hostilities, complete with satin wood inlay on the doors, and with carpets and rugs. Sir Douglas Haig, when he took over as Commander-in-Chief of the British Armies in France, also had a Rolls-Royce, as indeed did General Joffre, the French Commander. It would seem that the French, at least at very senior level, knew something about the magic of these British motor cars!

My father had to return to India and took his secretary Miss Thornton with him, but they were torpedoed in the SS *Persia* in the Mediterranean, and Eleanor drowned. It was a sad end to a long and loving friendship, which had produced not just the Spirit of Ecstasy, but also a child. When Lord Montagu eventually returned he took his Rolls-Royce along too. It was a rather different Rolls-Royce to the norm, with a new mascot, also created by Charles Sykes, called 'Silence and Speed' or nowadays 'Whisperer'. With his car, aide and his chauffeur, Brigadier-General John Walter Edward Douglas-Scott-Montagu, 2nd Baron Montagu, was able to return to the North-West Frontier to see the fruits of his labours.

This was the first war the British had known for decades where the misery and horror had been brought home. Here, sacrifices had to be made as well. The inroads on British shipping made by the unrestricted U-Boat campaign of 1917 onwards brought the first real rationing Britain had ever known. One thing in short supply was fuel; petrol had to be imported, and what did come in was needed for the cars, lorries, tanks and aircraft in France. The British, however, did not lack coal and the means of making coal-gas. The majority of big engines which powered munitions plants ran on gas, and there was no reason why cars at home could not be adapted to work on the same principle. Hence the Maxwell car of 1917, motoring around town with a huge ungainly gasbag atop. At the speeds it was asked to travel, aerodynamic considerations probably did not

My father in India with his Rolls-Royce.

apply, even if the designers had realised them, but what used to happen to these little cars when a stiff breeze was blowing from one side, and they tried to corner?

One of the best innovations of the Great War was the motorised ambulance. It could get wounded men from the battlefield back to the field hospital more quickly and in far more comfort than a horse-drawn cart. Studded tyres were fitted on one side, widely ribbed tyres on the other, to help the driver find some sort of grip. Many of the ambulances were built on Daimler chassis, the same firm that had the Royal Warrant to supply cars to His Majesty. Daimlers, in fact, were

everywhere, not just as ambulances, but also as tenders, ammunition trucks, and tow-lorries. The Prince of Wales, on an inspection at the Front, is reported to have drily observed, 'It seems to me the Daimler people are running this war'! On the other side of the Line, German staff officers were being driven about in the German Daimlers (which were called Mercedes by this time) that came from the original plant at Stuttgart. On both sides of the trenches also, despatch riders hurried to and fro on their motorcycles, taking orders to regiments in the Line.

The First World War brought the idea of motorised transport and motoring to ordinary people, and those people were not just men. Women, too began to drive for the first time in appreciable numbers as the war bit into the

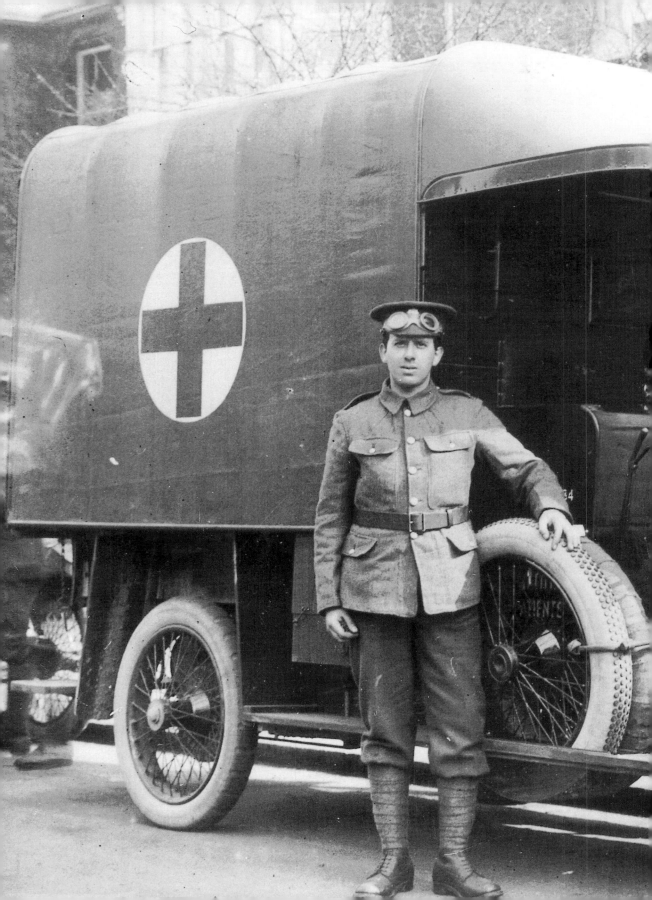

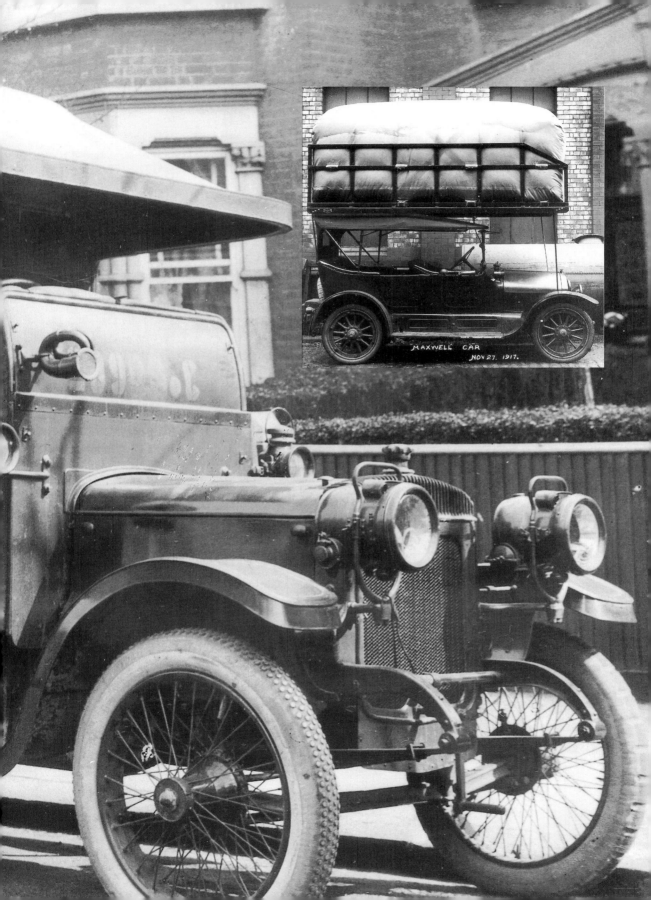

MAXWELL CAR
NOV 27. 1917.

▲ This particular lady is working on the exposed tappet push rods of a 1915 Buick truck, which must have needed all the muscle she possessed to turn over on the starting handle.

nation's manpower reserves. It was a move that would result after the war in women finally being treated more equally, even though they remained second-class citizens for many years. The authorities realised that women could do all sorts of mens' work, be it making shells and cartridges in the factories, taking over at the lathe or the press, replacing chauffeurs on the homefront, or even driving buses and ambulances.

There were three or perhaps four feats of

◄ The Daimler Ambulance, and driver.

◄ (Inset) Desperate times brought desperate remedies. The shortage of petrol meant that some cars were converted to run on gas, hence this Maxwell car of 1917, complete with an enormous gas balloon.

motoring, or at least motorised transport, that captured the imagination of the British during the First World War, and they all had their effects in future years. First, the way in which London buses were used to transport the men of the British Expeditionary Force to their great battle at Mons. Not even the railways could have done such a difficult task, though in the Twenties, outings by bus or coach — the original charabanc — would become commonplace. A similar feat was brought about by the Military Governor of Paris, General Gallieni, when he used Parisian Renault taxis to take the troops from his garrison to stiffen the French Army at the Marne. It was realised that the car could take small groups of people almost anywhere, and again in the Twenties, people would use the car to travel where they liked, when they liked. After the Great War, Britons would never again be total slaves to the railways and to the Bradshaw guide! The third feat was the mechanisation of the Forces, which allowed ordinary people to drive motor cars and lorries, and even, thanks to Mr Churchill's efforts at the Admiralty, aboard the giant tracked armoured vehicles which he called tanks. When the Second World War broke out 21 years later, many Britons knew they would be driving to war and not marching.

If Churchill, by his encouragement of the development of the tank, qualifies as one of the honorary British motorists of the war, then the other must be Colonel Lawrence. My father certainly helped to create the armoured car units, but it was Lawrence and his men, using their Rolls-Royces to charge up to and harass the Turk in the desert, who made the car at war glamorous. In a war where cold and damp and mud were everyday facts of life in the trenches, the desert war, with its camels, horses, and Rolls-Royces could seem almost enjoyable.

►King George V reviews the officers and men of the Royal Scots. His Majesty is being driven in a War Office Vauxhall, a popular staff car in World War One.

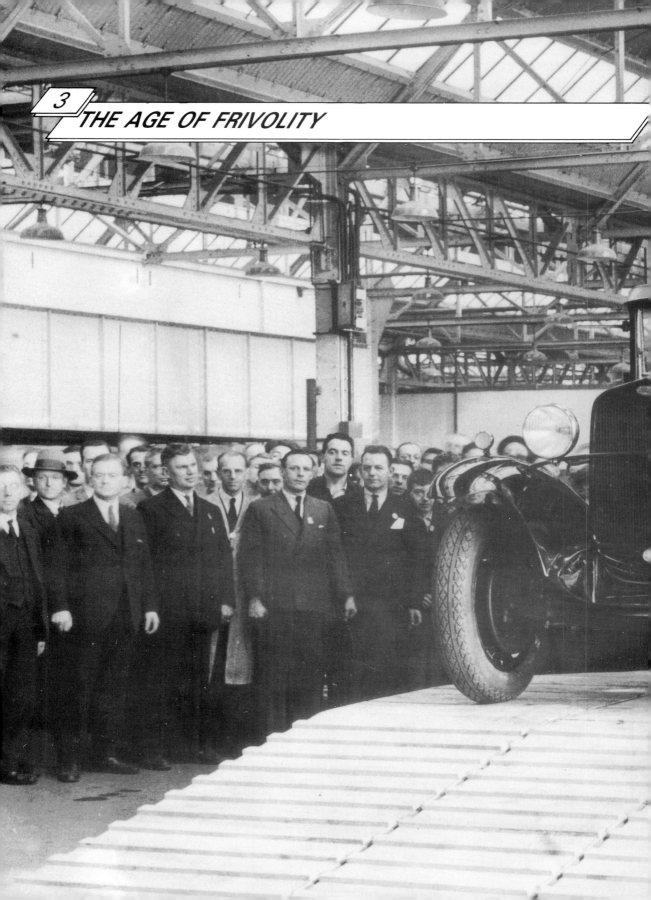

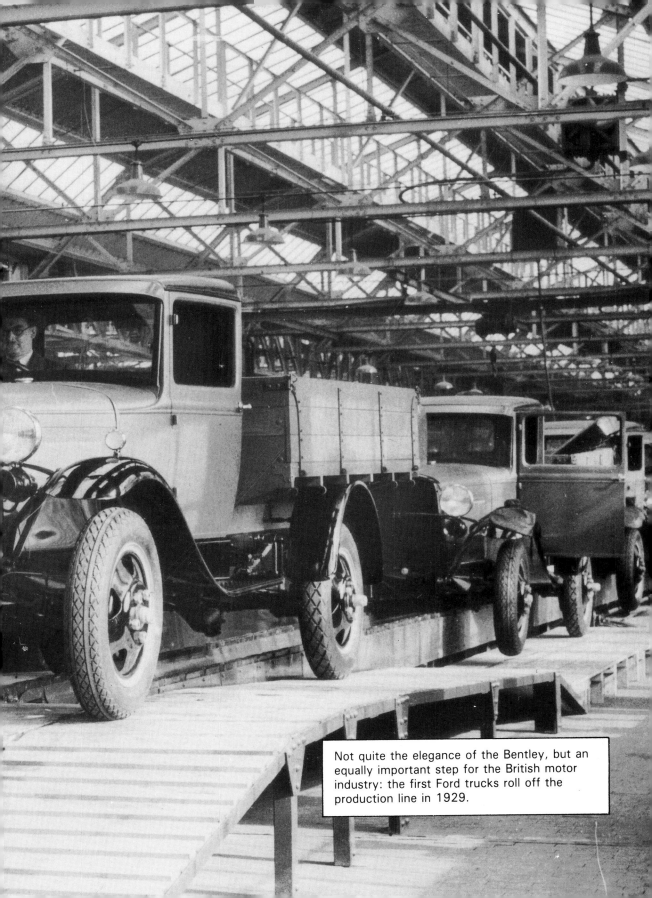

Not quite the elegance of the Bentley, but an equally important step for the British motor industry: the first Ford trucks roll off the production line in 1929.

On the eleventh day of the eleventh month at eleven o'clock, the firing died away along the Western Front. The men came home from the trenches. Some, it is true, went off to fight alongside the White Russians against the Bolsheviks. Others, who had survived the carnage of the war, came back, only to succumb to the great influenza epidemic that swept Europe as a sort of trailing 'Fourth Horseman'; indeed more people lost their lives as a result of the disease than were killed during the whole of the 1914-18 conflict. But to those who did survive pestilence and who had survived privation and war, the coming of peace heralded a new era. Fun and laughter, frivolity and pleasure, were to be had, provided you possessed at least a modest income. The Twenties roared into being.

It was a chance for all the small firms that had sprung up or achieved a certain prosperity from war to look for ways of making money from peace. And since many of the men who ran those companies had worked in engineering, cars and transport seemed a good way to make money. The large firms also looked forward to a return to their old business; companies like Rolls-Royce and Daimler, Napier, Vauxhall, Humber, Ford, Rover, Wolseley and Austin realised that the days of fat War Office contracts were over. But they knew now that the market was bound to be bigger than in the pre-war years; many men and women had had to drive during the war, some at least might well have acquired a taste for it. Thus the companies reasoned, and their hypothesis was based on sound facts. Many new companies were formed, and subsequently many were to collapse.

A lot of the men who came back from war had developed a taste for excitement; they had survived the gas and the shells and the bullets, and to many, the war had provided thrills and excitement they had never known before. It may seem odd to suggest that war has its thrilling moments — death and crippling injury do not seem very exciting — but many, principally the officers and gentlemen, did crave some sort of stimulus, be it hot jazz dancing, or driving sports cars at high speed. The ranks, or rather the ex-rankers now, wanted to drive too. It might be just a motorbike that they could afford with their war gratuities or demob money, or a very small car, but they too wanted the mobility, the means to escape and the excitement. Against that sort of background, it was not surprising that vehicle ownership spread steadily through the decade.

The officers and gentlemen now no longer in the service of His Majesty were naturally enough the men who stood out from the rest of the throng. Many of them kept their wartime ranks, even when out record-breaking or winning at Le Mans or Brooklands. They had already done their bit for the King and Empire, but it seemed they wanted to do that little bit more. As in cricket, rugger, athletics, so too motor sport: 'Play up, and play the game', was the slogan. In motor sport Britain found a whole host of heroes. Men like Captain Malcolm Campbell, Captain Sir Henry Birkin Bt, Major H.O.D. Segrave, and Captain Woolf Barnato, rushing out in their Bluebirds, Bentleys and Golden Arrows to triumph for Britain. Drivers like Frank Clement, Dr Benjafield, Lieutenant-Commander Glen Kidston, the brothers Clive and Jack Dunfee, S.C.H. 'Sammy' Davis, were all men of great courage who raced for the Bentley team in huge, monster motor cars, resplendent in their British racing green. And after the pantheon of great heroes, the little men who made them great. Walter Hassan, the mechanic who took over at the wheel of a record-attempt-making Bentley when everyone else gave up, and nearly killed himself trying to keep the speed for the honour of the team.

But motor sport is only part of the story of the 1920s British motorist, because though anyone with a car could take it to Brooklands and on payment of a fee drive round the track to emulate the heroes, it was not all about speed, and victories, and lap-times and record-breaking runs. It was the 1920s where ordinary people went driving. Purists may scoff, but I would venture to say that the cars of the 1920s in Britain were not the 4½-litre supercharged 'blower' Bentley, nor the Rolls-Royce Phantoms. The British cars of the 1920s were the Bullnose Morris and the Austin Seven, and the cars and social changes that sprang from them made the decade.

So we should now turn our attention not to the racers and record-breakers, nor to the great cars,

The Long Arm and Fat Tummy of the Law: two policemen at Brooklands shortly after the great motor track opened. Police and motorists quickly took up adverserial roles, positions they have never lost to this day!

The Standard plant at Canley in 1920: no sign of an assembly line here, just bits and pieces being produced and then assembled into motor cars.

but to two very interesting men: Herbert Austin and William Morris. Victorians, they had grown up in an age where order was everything, and where the British way of life was considered to be the most perfect in the world. Queen Victoria had presided over the greatest Empire the world had ever known; her soldiers and ministers had extended British rule around the globe, producing the Empire where 'the sun never set'. But the

whole Empire was founded at its roots on solid engineering achievement and industrial excellence. The British knew about mass quality production long before Henry Ford was born. What Ford had done, though, was to bring mass production to making cars. He took up the idea of the assembly line, turning out cars as no-one had managed to do before. By 1913, Ford in Britain was producing 6,000 cars a year, a small amount by modern standards but quite enough to make the firm Britain's biggest car maker. In the 1920s Austin and Morris set out to do the same.

Both men had joined the transport business early on. Austin had worked for the Wolseley company

before the turn of the century when that firm was better known as a manufacturer of agricultural equipment. Austin was Wolseley's chief engineer, and he saw the potential that the new motor car had to offer. So he had designed and built the first Wolseley cars, and in one of them had successfully completed the 1900 One Thousand Mile Reliability Trial along with C.S. Rolls, S.F. Edge and John Montagu.

For the next six years, Austin designed and built and undertook the manufacture of successive Wolseley cars. There are several Wolseleys among the entrants each year in the London to Brighton run. By 1906, though, Austin had tired

of working for others; he split away from the venerable Wolseley company and began to build cars on his own account. Wolseley, however, continued in production for many years on their own, before being absorbed into the empire of Mr Morris, the Nuffield Organisation, and becoming up-market versions of Morris products. The Wolseley, with its classic illuminated radiator sign, and quiet air of luxury, was well worth owning in the Forties, Fifties and Sixties. But Austin became a name all by itself.

Before the First World War, Austin built some large cars. There still exists a magnificent bright red Austin Racer built for the 1908 Grand Prix.

Having fun with a car in the age of frivolity meant a car with running boards, a stock of booze, and a girl to share it with!

Then came a smaller car, and a smaller one again, before the company got involved in production for the war effort. When the war was over, Austin decided to make a car suitable for the peacetime market. However, he made a big marketing mistake, something that would be repeated down the decades by his successors in the British motor industry. Herbert Austin put into production the Austin Twenty. It was the wrong car at the wrong time. It was heavy, it was dull and it did not sell — at least not in the numbers that Austin needed to stay in business. Austin had tried to adapt the American-style car to suit British needs and it would be a brave man who tried to do that today. It failed. Then Austin had a moment of pure genius; he worked out on the back of an envelope that what the ordinary person really wanted was a small, reliable and affordable car, able to carry

a family of four. It should be safe, it should be steady and above all, it should be lovable. If you could make a car like this, Austin thought, it might sell like wildfire and corner the market. The result was that tiny, spindly motor car, with silly little wheels, small seats, the minimum of luxury, but the maximum of affection, not just in Britain, but right around the world — the Austin Seven.

Nowadays we are used to best-sellers in the car world. The Volkswagen Beetle, still in production in Mexico and Brazil, the Citroen Deux Chevaux, with decades of manufacture behind it. In Britain, the Mini, the Ford Cortina and Ford Escort have all set records for sales and production. And in the 1920s, the Ford Model T had already scooped all the records of that sort worth having. But the Seven was something very different. It had a 747cc four-cylinder engine, a three-speed gearbox and weighed less than eight hundredweight. The hood worked in just the same way as that of the pram of the day; indeed, with a wheel at each corner, tiny springs, lamps not much bigger than those of a bicycle, the Austin Seven looked, and at times felt, like a toy. But it was no toy. In the hands of Gordon England, a racing driver and flyer of note, the new Seven took all the 750cc class records down at Brooklands. Thus Herbert Austin could launch his new car, with a top speed in racing guise of over 75 miles per hour, though 50 was the more usual strained, screaming maximum in road-going versions. It had four-wheel brakes, something which even the Rolls-Royce of the time did not possess, and it was cheap. It first emerged in 1922, to be reviewed with enthusiasm by *The Autocar*. The world's oldest motoring magazine trumpeted about its perfect road-holding, and the steering, for which the magazine had 'unstinted praise'.

The Seven could be made in vast numbers, and as production picked up, so the price came down. In 1928, a special version with a sunshine roof, the Austin Seven England Sunshine Saloon — a long name for a little car — could be had for £170. A year later, the standard car was selling at £140,

▶The Tortoise and the Hare: a Baby Austin racing a giant Bentley at Brooklands. Because of the handicapping system, the Austin had a very good chance of being placed first!

with a two seater version at £130. And nine years after that, the little car had crept down in price to £112. In the 16 years of mass production, Sir Herbert would produce 300,000 Austin Sevens, in a most staggering series of models and guises.

The Austin Seven, with a great deal of help from the handicapper, could race against even a mighty Bentley on the Brooklands circuit, and acquit itself well. It was made under licence in France, in Germany, and in Japan. It was even manufactured and sold in the United States, first under the name American Austin and then Bantam, though a Laurel and Hardy cartoon (where Olly tried to fit himself inside the car — and failed) made it little more than a figure of fun. But the British took the baby car to their hearts. It was modest and rather diffident, almost shy. Even today, the Seven retains its appeal, and the events organised by the various owners' clubs are among the most enjoyable in the motoring calendar.

While Austin was designing, building and selling his 'toy', Mr Morris was busy too. He was an Oxford garage proprietor selling cycles and cars when he entered the manufacturing business. In those days a great injection of capital to start a business like car building was not necessary — you just got the bits you thought you needed in one place, and put the thing together. William Morris delivered his first car in March 1913, and production began the same year. 393 had been sold by the end of the year. Despite the set-backs of the war, the Bullnose Morris — so-called because of its prominent brass radiator — began to sell. Once the war was over, Morris looked for great things, and in the month of October 1920 he sold 288 cars; by March 1921 the figure was up to 377. Then came a slump, which hit Morris just as badly as it hit Herbert Austin. Sales dived. Morris had nerve, and he had vision. Just as Austin was looking to produce a cheap small car, Morris realised he had to cut his prices, whatever the effect on his profits. So down came the price of the Bullnose Morris Cowley, from £525 to £425. Maybe he was lucky, maybe he was genius enough to do the right thing at the right price, but up went sales, up went production and up went Mr Morris's profits. By 1925, his factory was turning out 54,000 Bullnose Morris Cowleys a year, and

had become the major force in the British car industry. Other firms, like Rolls-Royce, Bentley and Lanchester might have more illustrious customers, but Austin and Morris put Britain on the road.

The products of Mr Morris spawned another great British car company; Morris Garages — one of the parts of Mr Morris's empire — took the bits that were used to make the Morris cars and turned out sporting versions of them. The initials MG and the traditional octagonal badge and instruments became an intimate part of British life. In the Seventies, MG advertising featured a young girl being driven at speed in an MG with the slogan, 'Your mother wouldn't like it'. She probably had.

Still, if these were the cars which were putting the British on to the roads in ever increasing numbers, it was the great names that were capturing the headlines: Sunbeam, Rolls-Royce, Bentley, Daimler and Lanchester were all great marques of the 1920s, making heavy, powerful, motor cars with pedigree. Quite often that pedigree was founded on motor sport, and for the age of frivolity, there was one name which led all the rest.

'The fastest lorries in the world' was the jibe which Ettore Bugatti threw at the products which came from a factory in Cricklewood, North London. They were great big motor cars, almost locomotive-like in size and strength. Yet they were lively and fast, fast enough to race. In the 1920s, Bentleys would win Le Mans no less than five times, and the legend of the Bentley Boys would go right around the world.

Walter Owen Bentley, known to all as 'W.O.', first became famous with the Bentley rotary engine he designed for the aircraft of the Royal Naval Flying Service and the Royal Flying Corps. It used aluminium extensively, a material which could be intricately worked, which was light, and which was thermo-dynamically efficient. Those Bentley engines were legendary, and when war ended, he was given the enormous sum of £8,000 by the Royal Commission on Awards. It was enough for him to put his own car company into being.

The first Bentley 3-litre engine saw the light of day in October 1919, in a first-floor room above

More than anything, owning a motor car meant
freedom to travel in the Twenties. It was perhaps
the best time to own a car: open roads and
wonderful scenery — without today's traffic jams.
This Bullnose Morris Cowley won 1st gold medal
on the London-Edinburgh rally.

a service station in Baker Street. Downstairs, Bentley and his brother were selling French D.F.P. cars; meanwhile the work was going on aloft using aluminium engine components to build the first Bentley. It took two further months before the first car was ready; in January 1920 it was road-tested by *The Autocar,* and as Hollywood might say, a star was born.

It helped, of course, that the man doing the road test was one of Bentley's oldest friends. Sammy Davis — Sidney Charles Houghton Davis to give him his full name — was sports editor of *The Autocar* and used to race motorbikes with W.O. outside the Bentley family home in Hampstead, much to the fury of Mr Bentley senior. Then Davis found himself as an Admiralty Inspector during the First World War, assessing his friend's new aircraft rotary engine. Who was more qualified to test the new car than someone who had grown up beside the man who built it? That was the way it was in those early days of motoring; there would be an outcry now if it were revealed, say, that the road test editor of *Motor* or *Autocar* was the best friend of the designer of the new Ford, or Jaguar. But then it seemed quite natural!

It is important to realise that when Davis drove this new British car, he was testing the first product of just one of literally dozens of companies which had sprung up with the intention of making cars after the Great War. Names like Clyno and Trojan, Crossley, Unic, Cubitt, ABC and Bean were all to be found on the fronts of cars being produced at the time, but few people remember them today. The Bentley was something different; it was fast and it was powerful, it was built to last and born to run.

The Twenties man-about-town took to the Bentley almost overnight, once sufficient finance had been raised to put the car into production. And fairly soon after that, a Captain Duff took an early 3-litre Bentley to a race in north-western France at Le Mans, then in its very first year. Today, the Le Mans 24-hour race is the toughest motor race in the world. It is fought out at speeds of over 220 miles per hour, and the winning cars expect to cover close on 3,000 miles during the course of the race. In the Twenties it was even tougher. True, the cars could achieve nothing like the top

speeds of the works' Porsches who have dominated the event in recent years. But the conditions the early racers competed under were quite appalling. It was the Bentleys' ability to withstand the pressure which made the car legendary. Bentleys did not win that first Le Mans in 1923, but they won in 1924, and then took the race four times running, from 1927 through to 1930. The following year, the company would be broke, and Rolls-Royce would buy it. But in just 12 years, Bentley Motors established a record of sporting legend that has still not been rivalled, except perhaps by Jaguar. It was the classic British notion of 'team spirit': mechanics, drivers, and bosses in the pits, fighting the race and the other competitors to win for Britain, and then being rather quiet and modest about it afterwards.

Bentley completed his original engineering training with the Great Northern Railway, as a premium apprentice — which meant that his father had paid for him to be there — at the great railway workshops in Doncaster. His hero, or one of them, was Sir Nigel Gresley, the great locomotive engineer, and Bentley based the design and construction of his cars on the sound railway engineering principles he was taught. Many experts have pointed out the similarity between the chassis of a Bentley, especially the 4½-litre version, and standard railway construction practice for wagons and goods vans. Bentley's cars were solidly built, with a clear concept as to what they were, and what they were meant to do. Bentley had already taken his cars to compete in the Tourist Trophy races on the Isle of Man before he tackled Le Mans. He had also sent a car to run in an early Indianapolis 500 race. Though reluctant at first to try Le Mans, he soon realised the reputation to be gained, provided his cars could win.

At which point, enter again a British motoring pioneer of the 1920s. Sammy Davis was really a professional driver, despite his full-time job at *The Autocar.* He knew all about cars, all about racing, and all about winning. In 1926 he was in a position to win the Le Mans race, but the Bentley snagged in the sand at one of the final corners, when it apparently ran out of brakes. But the following year, Davis wrote himself into motoring

Nothing much like this for the Le Mans race, but without heaters Twenties' motoring could be a chilly business for the amateur enthusiast and passenger!

legend, along with his race partner Dr Benjafield, by winning the 24-hour race in particularly heroic circumstances.

Davis and Benjafield were that year in the third of the three Bentley cars entered for the race. Theirs was 'only' a 3-litre Bentley; the other two team cars were the new 4½-litre models. As night fell across the Le Mans circuit, the three Bentleys were leading one, two and three. All was running smoothly, like a well-run railway. Bentley, in the pits, was making sure his cars ran on time. The

conditions were grim; early electric lights were insufficient to pick out fully the horrors of the dirt road. As the first two Bentleys rounded White House corner they came across a horror; a Schneider car had skidded and was blocking the road. The first Bentley went straight into it and the second followed suit. By a miracle, neither driver was badly injured, George Duller, a noted amateur steeplechase jockey, opting to jump for his life when he realised what was about to happen. The track was totally blocked when round the corner came the third Bentley, driven by Davis. His car was Number Three in the race records; in the Bentley pit, though, it was known as Old Number Seven, after the designation it had carried in the previous year's race. Davis had a premonition that something was wrong as he entered the bend at a speed of well over 70 miles per hour. He caught sight of bits of shattered fencing on the road, and stood on the brakes, hauling on the handbrake on the right-hand side of the car to slow down by as much as he could. It was not quite enough and the car smashed into the wreckage. Davis, amazingly, was more or less unhurt. The three Bentley drivers stood there discussing what to do, and then Davis realised, that despite the smash and the crazy appearance of his car, it could still actually run. Somehow he got the car back to the pit, made emergency repairs, and set off again.

The brakes came on in the oddest way, slewing the car at corners, but Davis and Benjafield found they could drive it after a fashion, and so with its wings buckled and headlamps pointing all over the place, the Bentley continued through the night. As the race wore on, it became obvious that there were just two cars in it: the crippled Bentley, and a French car, an Aries driven by Jean Chassagne. The cars were running neck and neck, but eventually the Aries overheated, and the big green Bentley, with its Union Flag painted like a battle ensign on each side, came through to win.

It was a classic British victory, and the Press went wild about it. The *Daily Mail* called it a wonderful triumph for British engineering skill. The paper went on to assert that 'There are no cars in the world to equal those of British manufacture in the quality and strength both of

Birkin, winning Le Mans with another Bentley in second place in 1929. It was a hat-trick, and it cemented their reputation as the greatest racing team of the age.

(*Inset*) W.O. Bentley and Sir Henry 'Tim' Birkin, posing in front of one of the great Bentley racers of the Twenties, looking intensely serious: Bentley with his slightly round tum, and Birkin with his fists tightly clenched. The year is 1929; when Birkin and Woolf Barnato drove the winning car at Le Mans.

engine and chassis'. They might have added something about the drivers. After the race, Davis discovered that the link arm to the steering was all but sheered through. A mere quarter inch of damaged, bruised metal was all that had stood between victory and disaster. For with the car running at up to 90 miles per hour, it would have meant certain death to either of the drivers had the link arm parted.

Davis — and his worthy co-driver Dr Benjafield — were by no means the only British Bentley heroes. Captain Woolf Barnato, chairman of the Bentley company in its last few years, drove brilliantly to win the Le Mans race three times, an achievement only surpassed by one other Briton, Derek Bell, in 1986. Barnato also found time to set up one of the great motoring legends, racing the Blue Train from the South of France, and like all the Bentley Boys, he was to be found racing regularly at Brooklands.

The other giant Bentley hero was 'Tim' Birkin. Captain Sir Henry Birkin Bt was the kind of fighting gamecock that the British produce at regular intervals. He was a real aristocrat, duck shooting and steeplechasing when he was not motor racing. He partnered Barnato when the Bentleys won the 1929 Le Mans Race, but it is his achievement in a race he never finished that deserves real praise. Birkin had taken it into his head that W.O. Bentley's basic design and concept of a racing car could be improved. He believed that it would be possible to take a 4½-litre Bentley and supercharge it to give better performance than the 6½-litre Bentley Speed Six which Bentley was using for the Le Mans team cars. The argument still continues. Bentley enthusiasts contest the issue to the present day, and will probably go on doing it for as long as the Bentley Drivers' Club exists. Birkin got together with the Hon. Dorothy Paget to get the money to finance his theory, and brought in designer Amherst Villiers to make the supercharger required. One of those blower Bentleys still greets visitors to the National Motor Museum. It is everything you could imagine . . . big, green, monstrously powerful . . . and Birkin used just such a car to write himself into history.

His moment came at the 1930 Le Mans Race. After a hat-trick of victories since 1927, one might imagine this was going to be a Bentley benefit. In fact, there had been concern that continued Bentley — and British — dominance of the event had been affecting the size of the crowds who attended this sort of French version of the Rio carnival once a year. But there was a strong possibility that the Bentleys might not make it, in the shape of the great German driver Rudolf Caracciola and a giant 7-litre supercharged Mercedes. You could not underestimate the challenge, nor the feelings of the nations thus set against one another.

The two Bentley teams, the official works team and Dorothy Paget's, decided that the Mercedes must be broken. Every possible effort should be made to lure the Mercedes up to speeds where something mechanical might fail. Caracciola was first away from the traditional Le Mans start, pursued by a pack of green Bentleys of all shapes and sizes, but suddenly, carving through his own team-mates, came Birkin in the supercharged 4½-litre. He set out to force the pace, putting in lap-speeds as fast as 87.13 miles per hour, and then a lap later just a few tenths of a second less than 90. All this on roads which would not be recognised today. On the long, bumpy Mulsanne straight, Birkin, risking his neck, simply flew past the Mercedes at what *The Autocar* reckoned to be 126 miles per hour. As *The Autocar* put it, 'What a car, and what a driver!'

Legend suggests that Birkin went one better than that, overtaking the huge German car on the grass rather than the road. And as the Bentley thundered, so it started to have trouble with its tyres. Strips of rubber tread simply flew off as the tyres struggled with the immense strain demanded of them. On the sixth lap, Birkin raced past the pits, with one of his rear tyres completely in shreds. He was driving at well over 110 miles per hour, possibly faster, in a car unable to handle any corner at speed. Amazingly he survived, and came into the pits to change the rogue wheel. The Mercedes gained a full lap, but slackened off, no doubt thinking the threat had passed. But in a further display of dramatic driving, Birkin caught up again and passed Caracciola. Once again he led, only for another tyre to burst. In all, the British car shed four tyres during that first furious

Above Why the horse lobby was frightened: an early steam coach puffs by, to the fury of the horsemen and their passengers alongside. Narrow interests combined with prejudice to force the steamers off the road, and set back the cause of mechanical road transport by half a century.

Below The first Daimlers to be offered for sale in Britain by the Great Horseless Carriage Company. They offered their cars as novelties to the nobility and gentry.

TO THE NOBILITY & GENTRY
MAY 1896

THE GREAT HORSELESS CARRIAGE Co Ltd

HAS THE HONOUR TO PRESENT

This NOVEL vehicle is propelled by an

INTERNAL COMBUSTION ENGINE

of 2 CYLINDERS and 6 HORSE POWER

relying on petroleum for its motive force

THE MECHANICAL carriage will attain the comfortable speed of

TWELVE MILES PER HOUR

on the level, while hills can be ascended and descended in safety

THE TWIN-CYLINDER 6 H.P. WAGONETTE

The Daimler Wagonette
is admirably suited to the needs of the
SPORTSMAN
AND LOVER OF THE COUNTRYSIDE,
giving as it does full facilities for the enjoyment of
FRESH AIR AND AN
UNINTERRUPTED VIEW OF THE Scenery

"A new mode of transport that has undoubtedly come to stay"
— VIDE DAILY PRESS

See Engraving

NO DUST
NO NOISE

'L'ENTENTE CORDIALE'

HUMBER

ENT AT STA HALL BY BENNETT BROTHERS LTD PRINTERS Nr BRISTOL

"BROWN" CARS

7 H.P. CHAIN DRIVEN
DOUBLE CYLINDER
8 H.P. GEAR DRIVEN
SINGLE CYLINDER
9 H.P. CHAIN DRIVEN
DOUBLE CYLINDER
12-14 H.P. CHAIN DRIVEN
FOUR CYLINDER
FULL PARTICULARS ON APPLICATION.

TRIAL
RUNS
BY
ARRANGEMENT.

THE BROWN
12-14 H.P. CAR.

BROWN·BROTHERS·LIMITED
HEAD OFFICES, GT. EASTERN ST. LONDON. E.C.   WEST END SHOWROOMS, 15. NEWMAN ST. OXFORD ST. W.
MANCHESTER. 269-273. DEANSGATE.   PARIS. 31. RUE DE LA FOLIE MÉRICOURT.

The Brown and the Humber: both cars of the Edwardian era, the Golden Age of motoring. Drivers and passengers in both cars were well wrapped up against the cold, while the Humber advert, which dates from just before the First World War, shows the lack of trust between motorists and the police which has sadly persisted down the years. Thankfully the proper Edwardian family could always call on the services of Nurse to distract the force of the Law!

The car of the age of discovery, and the shape of things to come on its bonnet. The car is the 1907 Rolls-Royce Silver Ghost, the car that made the reputation of the company. *Above* is the front cover of the 1907 Christmas issue of *The Car Illustrated*, the magazine my father founded.

CHRISTMAS NUMBER

Edited by THE CAR *Lord Montagu*

A JOURNAL OF TRAVEL
By LAND SEA and AIR

ILLUSTRATED.

CHARLES SYKES.

Towards the Dawn.

If the Rolls-Royce Silver Ghost was the car of the Edwardian age, the Bentley was the car that roared through the Twenties. *Above*, the famous Terence Cuneo painting of the Bentley Le Mans victory in 1924, and *below*, the famous 4½ litre supercharged Bentley. This car is among the collection at Beaulieu.

More than a
catalogue –

a guide to modern motoring

MORRIS 1933

STEP INSIDE FOR A FREE COPY

THE INTERNATIONAL TROPHY

1/= OFFICIAL PROGRAMME

BROOKLANDS
ON THE OCCASION OF THE SILVER JUBILEE
OF H. M. KING GEORGE V.
MONDAY, MAY 6th 1935
START 3 P.M.   DISTANCE 250 MILES.
Organised by: THE JUNIOR CAR CLUB.

Patron H.M. The King

MOTOR
EXHIBITION
CARS & BOATS

OCT. 17-26
OLYMPIA

Daily 10 till 10 - Admission 2/6
(EXCEPT THURSDAYS & TUESDAY BEFO! 5 – 5/-)

Motoring in the Thirties had an even wider appeal.
Austin and Morris were each running their empires,
selling strongly to the family man. A trip to the
Motor Show became an obligatory exercise for the
motoring enthusiast, while Brooklands offered a
continual programme of sprints and distance races.

The Austin Seven

Capt. Malcolm Campbell breaks World's Record at **206.95 Miles per Hour!** Using *Castrol*

DAYTONA BEACH, FEB. 19TH, 1928. CAPT. MALCOLM CAMPBELL, NAPIER-CAMPBELL "BLUE BIRD" BREAKING WORLD'S MILE RECORD.

AN ALL BRITISH TRIUMPH **207 Miles per Hour!** THE HIGHEST SPEED EVER ATTAINED ON LAND

On March 29th 1927, Major H. O. D. Segrave, driving a Sunbeam Car lubricated with Wakefield Castrol, broke World's Records for 1 Kilometre, 5 Kilometres and 1 Mile, reaching a speed of over 207 m.p.h. one way of the course.

Using WAKEFIELD *Castrol* MOTOR OIL

Away from the racetrack, the British dominated the battle for the Land Speed Record. Sir Malcolm Campbell and Sir Henry Segrave were the front runners, breaking the record time and again for Britain, the Empire and — as these famous adverts recall — for Castrol!

231 Miles per Hour! Wonderful Record of GOLDEN ARROW — The Highest Speed Ever Attained on Land

— Of Course Segrave used WAKEFIELD *Castrol* MOTOR OIL

DAYTONA BEACH, MARCH 11TH, 1929, MAJ. SIR HENRY SEGRAVE, IRVING-RAPIER SPECIAL "GOLDEN ARROW" BREAKING WORLD'S RECORD FOR 1 MILE AT 231·36 M.P.H.

70

Capt. MALCOLM CAMPBELL SHATTERS WORLD'S LAND SPEED RECORD!

245 M.P.H. ON THE NAPIER-CAMPBELL "BLUE-BIRD" USING... WAKEFIELD *Castrol* MOTOR OIL

THE PRODUCT OF AN ALL-BRITISH FIRM

1000 H.P. SUNBEAM
THE FIRST CAR IN THE WORLD
TO ATTAIN A SPEED
OF
OVER 200 M.P.H.

SUNBEAM

Today four of the famous record breaker cars are at the National Motor Museum. The front three are the two Sunbeams and Sir Henry Segrave's Golden Arrow. Behind is Donald Campbell's Bluebird, the last car to hold the 'proper' Land Speed Record.

71

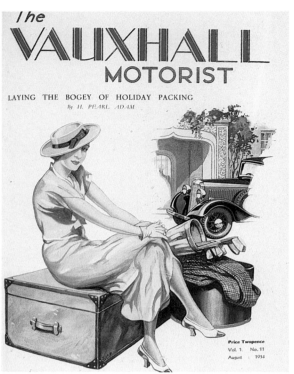

Owners' enthusiasm for their new cars was kept up by the manufacturers through their own magazines. It is doubtful whether the average Morris lady owner could even afford to go skiing, let alone take her car, but these sort of pictures bestowed a glamour on other people's everyday motoring.

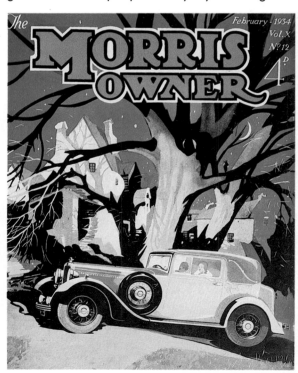

burst of driving, and Birkin drove himself into motor racing history. As the *Daily Mail* put it, the 'hero of the 24-hour endurance race here, which was won by the British Bentleys, was Capt. H.R.S. Birkin, who never finished'. The paper recounted how Captain Birkin had sacrificed his chance for his team. They might have said 'for his country' as well. The *Daily Express* also proclaimed the drama of the 'New British Speed Victory', applauding Birkin's 'Drive or Burst Decoy to Germans'. For Birkin, the duck-hunter, the role of decoy must have been quite fun. Later he would set a lap record at Brooklands in a specially streamlined version of the 4½-litre blower Bentley, and the outline of the Brooklands' 'Battleship' today forms the central emblem of Britain's top motoring club, the British Racing Drivers' Club. Birkin died in 1933 from septicaemia after being burnt on the arm at a race in Tripoli. He is buried in the churchyard at Blakeney on the north Norfolk coast, near the marshes he loved. Fifty years on, his grandson organised a memorial day, and cars with which Birkin was associated came from all over Britain. Among the men who attended were Amherst Villiers, the lean ascetic visionary who designed the supercharger, and Billy Rockell, one of the Birkin pit crew. The race incidentally was won by Woolf Barnato, partnered by Lieutenant-Commander Glen Kidston, of the Royal Navy. Caracciola's Mercedes broke under the strain of competition, as Bentley had planned.

The triumphs of Davis, Birkin and Barnato in their green Bentleys put the British centre-stage on the motor racing map. Since the Twenties, the British have regularly produced champion drivers and champion racing cars. It would take another two decades and another world war before the next spate of victories, those of Jaguar, but the sporting nature of the British driver was created by the Bentleys at Le Mans. They simply took the 'team spirit' and applied it to motor racing. And the fun they got up to off the track made them equally famous. After their triumph in the 1927 Le Mans race, Davis and Dr Benjafield were feted at a special dinner on the first floor of the Savoy. Toasts were made, exquisite course succeeded exquisite course, but one important guest was absent. Finally, the huge double doors at the end of the room were thrown open and Old Number Seven drove into the meal in a cloud of fumes and exhaust. The Bentley Boys had decided the car ought to be there, and manhandled it up the stairs into the dining room, to the horror of the Savoy staff and management, but to their own — and posterity's — delight.

Two men whose motoring equally attracted the limelight also contributed to the notion of the great British motorist. Captain Malcolm Campbell and Major Henry Segrave went in for the equally perilous but more solitary sport of record-breaking. Both men were motor racers too — Segrave, for example, won the 1923 French Grand Prix in a Sunbeam — but their greatest triumphs came when pushing speed to its limit. Segrave did his land speed records in Sunbeams, and then in the beautiful Golden Arrow, which together with two of the Sunbeams is proudly preserved at Beaulieu, at the National Motor Museum. Campbell did his record-breaking in a succession of cars, all called Bluebird. Both were knighted but Campbell was perhaps the luckier man. Segrave was killed attempting the world water speed record in the Thirties, Campbell survived the second war to die in the late Forties.

Segrave began his drive for records in 1926 using a special version of the V12 Sunbeam Tiger to set a record of over 152 miles per hour on the sands at Southport. The following year he journeyed to the sands at Daytona, in Florida, with another Sunbeam and almost at a stroke smashed through the record to set a new one in excess of 203 miles per hour, becoming the first man to exceed 200 miles per hour on land. An achievement surely to match Davis and Benjafield's victory that year at Le Mans. But Segrave had more to give. In 1929, he took the beautiful Golden Arrow back to America and set a new land speed record of 231.44 miles per hour. The car was designed around a huge Napier aero-engine, and its unusual shape was to streamline the curious style of the Napier machinery.

The man Segrave kept having to beat was Captain Malcolm Campbell. Campbell had served in the Royal Flying Corps in the Great War, and like Segrave, and indeed all those Bentley drivers,

Parry Thomas and the car in which he was killed — 'Babs'. It looked dangerous and it was: the crash on Pendine sands in Wales caused the great back-wheel driving chain to decapitate the driver.

(*Inset*) One of Britain's great motoring heroes: Major Segrave and the 1000 horsepower Sunbeam which first exceeded two hundred miles an hour. The car is one of four land speed cars at the National Motor Museum.

he remained attached to his military title. In a series of Bluebirds, Campbell kept raising the record; in the Thirties he would eventually top 300 miles per hour. But Segrave is remembered in another way; every year a special committee meets to decide which British or Commonwealth subject has, during the previous year, most clearly achieved distinction in their commitment to transport by land, air or sea. The person or persons selected, if an award is made, receive the Segrave Trophy at a special ceremony at the Royal Automobile Club in London. Previous winners have included flying ace Jean Batten, motorcycle champion Geoff Duke, and the entire Falklands Task Force. So Sir Henry Segrave's gallant and successful attempts on the land speed record earned him his place in the pantheon of British heroes.

A less fortunate man was Parry Thomas, killed when his record-breaker 'Babs' crashed on the Pendine sands in Wales. 'Babs' had none of the beauty of the Golden Arrow, nor of the Bluebirds in their various guises. It was a big 'Chitty-Chitty Bang-Bang' sort of car, using a large American Liberty engine to generate the power needed to raise the speed for the attempt. At any rate it was unsuccessful, and Parry Thomas was killed. The car was buried in the sands where it crashed: years later it was exhumed and restored.

The 1920s might mean speed and records and motor races to some, to others it was all about elegance. King George V and Queen Mary set the tone for the British nobility and gentry by ordering giant, stately Daimlers with bodywork by Hoopers. King George, whose sense of duty to his people was profound, insisted that his cars should have huge windows, and that the seats where he and Queen Mary sat should be raised

to permit their subjects to have a good look at their rulers. The cars, powered by sleeve-valve engines with a characteristic of silence, proceeded on their stately way, emitting gentle clouds of blue oil smoke!

King George V was, however, somewhat discreet about his cars. There was to be a minimum of chrome about the Royal Daimlers and even the radiator was painted black. But other potentates had no need or desire to be so reserved and restrained; the Rajahs, Maharajahs and Nizams of India realised their cars could enable them to be seen in the full — and as it would turn out — the final flush of their glory and splendour, and they provided plenty of employment for the luxury British car makers and the coach-builders associated with them by ordering motor cars as ornate and splendid as they were ostentatious.

The main difference between the cars of the Edwardian era and the cars of the Twenties — from an external point of view — was the development of the medium-sized saloon. The

▲The King and Queen at Hooper's inspecting their new car in 1924. It has the big windows the King insisted on to let his subjects get a good view of the King-Emperor.

▲▶The Maharajah of Alwar's fancy: a gold painted Lanchester with imposing state carriage bodywork for the Rajah and his passengers. At the height of the Arab oil boom, sheiks from the Middle East sought equally ostentatious vehicles from specialist car builders half a century on!

▶How my father planned the London-Birmingham route in the Twenties. Put in the central crash barrier, the third lane and the roundabout at the junction and you have how the road turned out when it was finally built.

Britain's first really great motor works was at Dagenham, built on the Thames amidst the Essex marshes. Later in the Second World War it would be camouflaged to resemble the marshland it had originally been!

increased power of the cars of the Twenties enabled smaller cars to carry the extra weight of the full-bodied cars, and that made it easier and more comfortable for travel. You did not need to race about in a 3-litre Bentley or a Vauxhall 30/98, exposed to the elements. You could travel in some style, provided you wrapped up well; in summer, the flappers could actually travel in the bright, skimpy clothes that had become fashionable. Luxury though, remained the key note of the up-market medium British cars, and the requisites for creating cocktails could be fitted with some style into a deep seat-back.

My father's major campaign during the 1920s was his effort to persuade a reluctant government to build the very first motorway. John Scott-Montagu could speak in Parliament as a member of the House of Lords, and he pushed hard for a motorway to link London and Birmingham. It would have had all kinds of consequences, especially for British manufacturing industry, but his effort was thwarted. It seemed that the British might accept cars, and applaud the victories and the records made and achieved by their racers and speed kings, but they did not want an M1. It took dictatorships in Europe to build the first motorways; Mussolini in Italy was able to appreciate the strategic use of a fine major road, and Hitler was ready to build and improve on that model, thus providing himself, and his re-created German Army, easy access to the frontiers. Britain remained true to the rolling English road. My father died on 30 March 1929, having seen the motor car develop from a joke and a nuisance into a part of the British way of life — even if it would not take motorways seriously!

Perhaps the biggest unseen change in British cars in the Twenties came in the way they were built. At the start of the decade, cars were built part by part. It had been done that way since motoring began, and as far as many car makers were concerned, it could go on that way. Mass production did develop; Morris and Austin converted gradually, while Ford, in spite of all the troubled news coming from the other side of the Atlantic, created their giant plant at Dagenham in Essex to make cars from scratch. The plant opened as the 'Roaring Twenties' drew to a close.

DEPRESSION AND RECESSION

Ever the showman, Malcolm Campbell poses with his latest Bluebird, a spotter aircraft, spectators and not a few policemen, prior to making one of his record-making races at the Salt Lake Flats in Utah. In 1935 Sir Malcolm became the first man to travel at over 300 miles an hour by car on land.

The Twenties had begun with a slump and ended with the worst depression the world had ever known. It was the dreadful 'Black Thursday' on Wall Street, home of the New York Stock Exchange, which triggered the world-wide collapse, though the signs of impending doom had been there for years for those who knew where to look. Vast expansion and speculation in the United States, together with the lack of inter-governmental controls, rendered the world economy particularly vulnerable, and when Wall Street went, the rest of the world went too. It was like Humpty-Dumpty bringing down not only the wall he sat on, but all the King's horses and all the King's men as well.

29 October 1929 was 'Black Thursday'. Investors suddenly and dramatically lost confidence in the stocks they were buying and selling, often 'on margin' or pure speculation. The prices started to drop, suddenly they were tumbling, and Wall Street had its biggest-ever single day fall, in real terms. Entrepreneurs saw their empires collapse. Some held their nerve, others panicked, one or two jumping from the skyscrapers which housed their offices. The effects of the depression spread quickly around the world. In Britain the dole queues lengthened, and the country began a slide towards political crisis which would result in the National Government. In Germany, the unsteadiness of the Weimar Republic daily became more obvious, and the economic crisis paved the way for Hitler and National Socialism to rise to power.

It heralded big changes too for the British motor industry and for British drivers. The Twenties had been bad enough, crushing one after another manufacturer. The onset of the age of depression and recession brought further casualties. First and still most mourned was the firm which more than any other had established the British motor sport tradition. Bentley Motors went down, with no-one ready or willing to put in more money, and a big institutional investor, the London Life Association, suddenly hauling in the reins. There was a chance the company might survive in some independent form, possibly still at its works at Cricklewood, when talks began with the Napier company based at Acton. Napier had moved away from car

manufacture into the production of aero-engines, but the possible merger never came to pass. Eventually Bentley Motors were absorbed within the Rolls-Royce empire, Bentley ceased to be an independent company, and W.O. Bentley himself found his design efforts frustrated. Bentleys would race no more at Le Mans as a company, and an era of heroes was suddenly at an end.

Almost, but not quite. The three-times Le Mans winner Woolf Barnato may not have been able to conduct the affairs of the Bentley firm with enough skill to avoid the crash, but he could still drive. His final great motoring feat was to race the fabled Blue Train from the south of France all the way to London. Driving a streamlined Bentley Speed Six coupé, Barnato roared north through France, stopping at specially set-up petrol dumps to refuel as he and his passengers hurtled through the night. They left the train for dead, and reached Victoria a full four hours before the express steamed in. It outraged the French authorities, who promptly banned Bentleys from exhibiting at the forthcoming French Motor Show.

It was a time of depression and recession, and a time of change. Sir Henry Royce, who had lived for most of the previous 15 years in the south of France, died in 1933. He had designed one truly great car, the Silver Ghost, and two magnificent sequels, the Phantom I and Phantom II. Sir Henry had worked himself so hard during the early years of the car that bore his and Charles Rolls' name, that at the insistence of his fellow directors, Royce moved first to West Wittering and then Le Canadel in the Riviera. It was a magnificent place to live and to work, but no doubt Royce missed the hubbub and the throb of the great factory. Royce himself won no races, entered no events and took part in no attempts on land speed records. Yet he established principles of motor car design and construction which gave Britain a lofty reputation around the world, and which, even today, are enough for Rolls-Royce Motors to sell plenty of cars!

One family that could afford Rolls-Royce but did not buy them — at least not for official purposes — was the House of Windsor. In the Thirties they stuck with tradition, continuing the close relationship with the Daimler company

Sir Henry Royce pictured in his final years at Le Canadel, his home in the south of France, next to a car many considered to be his greatest masterpiece, the Phantom II. Royce all but worked himself to death during the formative years of Rolls-Royce: it was the company's idea he should settle away from the plant, first at West Wittering in Sussex, then on the Riviera.

begun when my father had taken Edward, Prince of Wales, for that famous drive in the New Forest. King George V would often be seen leaving Buckingham Palace, the guardsman on sentry-duty loyally and smartly presenting arms, while the King-Emperor doffed his top hat to passers-by. This little bit of tradition has all but died out in the 1980s, though City gentlemen are sometimes to be seen raising their bowlers to the Lord Mayor when he or she drives through the City. The gesture is almost always returned. The royal Daimlers had their own very special mascots. No Flying Lady here; the Monarch's cars carried a sculpture of England's Patron Saint, St George, slaying the dragon. Those were the days

when the Guards mounted guard outside the Palace rather than inside as they do now.

The influence of the Daimler tradition on the British Royal Household was immense, and nowhere was it more obvious than at the Coronation of King George VI in 1937. Down Whitehall, from Trafalgar to Parliament Square, came a procession of Daimlers stretching as far as the eye could see, and all in line astern like a fleet of dreadnoughts! The Royal Family, by tradition, travelled by coach — the horse still ruled that part of British national life. But VIP's who needed to be in the procession on its way to the Abbey journeyed by motor rail. That was the first time it had happened at a British coronation.

Though King George VI was a stickler for formality, setting great store by appearance, the rest of the Royal Family were not quite so severe. The excitement over Prince Andrew's bride, Sarah, Duchess of York, was identical to that made over the last Duchess of York, fifty-five

83

▲The sentry presents arms as the King-Emperor leaves Buckingham Palace in a Royal Daimler to go racing at Newmarket in June 1931. In those days the sentry boxes were outside Buckingham Palace.

▶Coronation Day 1937: blue jackets of the Royal Navy line Whitehall as Daimlers — over thirty of them in this picture alone — make their way from the Palace to the Abbey for the Coronation of King George VI.

years ago. In 1932, the Duchess of York, later to become Queen and then Queen Elizabeth the Queen Mother, visited Brooklands and spent some time chatting to some of the competitors in the race. Fleet Street photographers scurried over looking for the best-possible camera angle as the Duchess, then, as in the Eighties, looking radiant, spoke to one of Britain's rising breed of women racing drivers, Mrs Tommy 'Bill' Wisdom. Mrs Wisdom, who would later in the decade compete at Le Mans and help check a new British car was ready for production by driving it to Baghdad, was about to compete in an Invicta car. It was all part of the change that was coming about in Britain, as motoring moved down through the classes and as women began to assert themselves. Mrs Wisdom and her husband, a celebrated motoring writer, competed as equals on the race-track. There is no record, however, of the future Queen Mother trying her hand behind the wheel of one of the Brooklands racers!

The motto of the Brooklands' track in those days was 'the right crowd and no crowding'. It was a splendid place to witness motor racing; one could come down by train from London, or of course drive down; there were plenty of places to snatch a cup of tea, and one could watch a vast chunk of the action from up on the hill in the lea of one of the corners of the circuit. Other visitors used punts or boats on the river Wey which flowed nearby. One of the most exciting sections of the huge banked circuit was by the railway line, which culminated in the infamous 'Brooklands Bump'. A car hitting this section would literally take off and fly, often for dozens of yards. Photographers swarmed to the point where the cars would hit the bump, to take some of the most exciting motor sport photographs of the era.

Brooklands never made money. Throughout the Thirties, there were fears about its future, and it

The Queen Mother as Duchess of York in 1932 chatting with Mrs Tommy 'Bill' Wisdom at Brooklands.

Le Mans again, and a lot of the interest in Le Mans disappeared as far as the British public were concerned. The same, incidentally, holds true today, when for the past few years the first eight or nine places have been taken by Porsches. One British driver, Derek Bell, has made history for a Briton by winning Le Mans four times, but he is not a household name in the way that Barnato and Birkin were in their day. Let us hope that British car makers get into their stride again and challenge at Le Mans with all-British teams, as the XJR6 Jaguar did in 1986. Then the British will treat the great 24-hour race with the respect and attention it deserves.

Which takes us back to Brooklands. Here the local residents objected to all-night racing, so the concept of the Double-Twelve was created. The drivers took part in a 24-hour race, split into two parts of 12 hours each. Overnight, the cars were kept in a special pound. The locals also objected to the noise, and so the special Brooklands silencer was created. This was an exhaust system which ended in a fish-tail shaped silencer, meant to limit the sound. In fact all it did was to give a special tone and pitch to the exhaust note. The noise was diminished, but the cars were still loud by the standards of the day, a day which knew no jets or Concorde!

The great danger at Brooklands was 'going over the top'; the giant racers were getting faster and faster and sooner or later one or other of them would go too fast for the steering or suspension and edge up off the top of the Brooklands banking to crash. Ideas were put forward; one notion suggested a sort of wooden catch fencing at the top, but in reality Brooklands was old and falling to bits. Sir Henry Birkin described it, shortly before his death, as the most dangerous, outworn and undesirable motor course in the world. The handicapping system meant he often had to tear round at speeds of 140 miles per hour to make sure he had done enough laps to beat an MG with a tiny top speed, which the handicapper had favoured.

The Thirties thus saw the decline of Brooklands as a serious motor racing circuit. Britain had not bothered with the various Grands Prix since the Sunbeams had competed so well in the Twenties,

was realised that it did not fit in with the continental approach to motor sport. Other countries had their banked tracks, but Brooklands was unique. It made a very British approach to motor sport possible within the United Kingdom, but it did not help the British in their efforts to compete in Europe with other countries. There was racing, too, at Crystal Palace, and at a new track at Donington in the Midlands, plus the hillclimbs like Shelsey Walsh which had always been part of the British motoring scene since the One Thousand Mile Reliability Trial had sent entrants up hills to prove the motor car's climbing power.

The British had also got out of step with the sort of cars needed for the Le Mans 24-hour race which was no longer a benefit outing for the British Bentleys. Tim Birkin and Lord Howe won the race in 1931, driving an Alfa-Romeo — an Italian car! During the Thirties, a British car won Le Mans just once; a 4½-litre Lagonda Rapide, driven by John Hindmarsh and Louis Fontes, and that was scarcely an all-British triumph. It was to be 1951 before British drivers, driving a British car, won

and there was nothing British that could be altered successfully to take part. Raymond Mays, a sportsman who took part in hill-climbs, tried to remedy the lack by forming ERA — English Racing Automobiles. They were neat little cars, but they were not big enough to take part in the big events. For those, you needed real money, and that was not forthcoming in Britain with three million people out of work and the depression in full, agonising swing.

In Germany, priorities were rather different. The country had more people than in Britain out of work, and an economy in deeper trouble. Adolf

'The Right Crowd and No Crowding' was the slogan which brought spectators to see the British Racing Drivers Club 500 Mile Race at Brooklands in September 1932. By then the old track was becoming very worn indeed as may be noticed from the patching.

Dick Seaman pictured with the Nazis having won for Mercedes in the German Grand Prix of 1938. He looks less than delighted at the Nazi ritual.

Hitler had just taken over the Government, and was busy establishing National Socialist — Nazi — policies in all areas of work and play. He reasoned that an all-conquering German motor racing team would carry German — and more importantly Nazi — reputation around the world. Hitler, therefore, pumped thousands of marks into the two great German racing teams, Mercedes and the Auto-Union, a grouping of several medium-sized German car firms' race teams. The new cars were quite unlike anything that had gone before, low-slung, with enormous power on tap. The Mercedes followed relatively standard procedure: an engine at the front driving the back wheels, but the Auto-Union put their engine behind the driver, and created a sensation; huge engines, sometimes

of V12, sometimes V16 configuration, pouring the power down through quite narrow wheels onto the track. There was quite simply nothing like them and they were all-conquering.

A young British driver, Richard Seaman, joined the Mercedes team in the late Thirties. It was a difficult time — in hindsight the wrong time — because he found he was racing under the Swastika to glorify the Nazi Party. He was a great driver, but it cannot have been easy for him, racing under a Nazi regime dedicated to promoting German genius and ability. He won the German Grand Prix in 1938 at the Nurburgring, a giant motor racing circuit built originally to provide employment in the local area, and then to test and race cars. It must have been a great triumph, but on the victor's podium he was faced with a sea of Nazi salutes. He himself produced something between a salute and a wave. Seaman was fatally injured shortly afterwards in a race at Spa in Belgium when he crashed in the wet. Dragged from the blazing wreckage of the car, he died in hospital.

Seaman's involvement with the mighty Mercedes team was just one sign of the way the British car makers had fallen behind in motor sport. Brooklands and the hill-climbs were all very well in their way, but when the Mercedes and Auto-Union cars came to Donington in 1937, the huge gap that had opened up was suddenly, painfully obvious. These huge racers, hurtling around the track, the most powerful Grand Prix cars ever made, were invincible. British engineering excellence, so praised at the end of the Twenties after the Le Mans Bentley victories, had failed to keep pace. In the war that followed, Britain was lucky that two aero-engineers, Sydney Camm and R.J. Mitchell, had managed to stay the odd step ahead of the designers at Messerschmitt to build, fly and produce the Hurricane and Spitfire! Rolls-Royce were involved in the production also.

▶Brooklands was also used for record attempts till well into the 1930s. This was the moment — here recorded in print — when John Cobb, driving the Napier-Railton took the lap record for the track. The massive car is still in existence and is regularly produced at vintage events.

Page
—256—

October
—1935—

STOP PRESS !

JOHN COBB RECAPTURES THE BROOKLANDS LAP RECORD AT 143.44 M.P.H.

FLYING KILOMETRE COVERED AT 151.97 M.P.H.

The Napier-Railton at speed on the Home Banking

JOHN COBB

JOHN COBB again holds the Brooklands Lap Record !

On Monday, October 7th, he took his giant Napier-Railton out determined to wrest the Brooklands Lap Record from the holder, Oliver Bertram, whose account of his own exploits appears on pages 264 and 265 of this issue.

Cobb's best lap was 143.44 m.p.h. which bettered the existing figure by some half a mile an hour.

During this effort, John Cobb exceeded the fastest speed ever previously set up at Brooklands, by covering the flying kilometre at 151.97 miles an hour—a speed which, but a few years ago, would have been sufficient to lift the world's land speed record !

Following closely on his win in the 500 Miles Race, reported on pages 247-250 of this issue of SPEED, and his fine achievements at Salduro, this new success of Cobb's must make 1935 a very memorable year for him.

In addition to demonstrating the splendid design and workmanship characteristic of this car, Cobb has now made a gesture which must silence for all time those critics of Brooklands who maintain that the Track is unfit for use by cars with a potential speed of more than 120 m.p.h.

Brooklands finally closed when war came in 1939, the banking being camouflaged by trees and shrubs, whose roots ate into the concrete and finished what man had begun. The place did sterling work during the war, for Barnes Wallis, the inventor of the 'bouncing bomb' designed his Tallboy and Grand Slam bombs here, using the old clubhouse as his offices. Two replicas of the giant bombs stand there today. In the Sixties and Seventies, Brooklands was home to the VC10 aircraft, built and completed there. Today what is left of the place is a living museum to early motoring and early aviation. But the site today is very different as the buildings of the Brooklands Industrial Park and the present Gallaher factory hide much of what Brooklands once was.

One man deeply involved financially with Brooklands in its declining years was Sir Malcolm Campbell. In 1932 he raised the land speed record to over 250 miles per hour. Three years later, this undoubtedly heroic man blasted through the 300 mile per hour figure with a fully streamlined version of his Bluebird car, on the salt flats at Utah. Then he retired, leaving two other Britons to take on the quest for speed. John Cobb and Captain George Eyston would contest the record all the way to the outbreak of war, in just the same way as Segrave and Campbell had. The two men duly obliged, with Cobb lifting the record to over 350 miles per hour in 1938, and to just under 400 after the war. Cobb, like Segrave before him, and like Sir Malcolm's son Donald Campbell after him, was killed going for the world water speed record, his boat Crusader crashing on Loch Ness. But the Thirties, and for that matter all those inter-war years, were years of triumph for Britain when it came to the land speed record. Segrave, taking on the mantle from the first post-war British record holder, Kenelm Lee Guinness, Parry Thomas, then Campbell, Eyston and Cobb.

In 1983 the man who won the land speed record back for Britain, Richard Noble, was proud to admit that his early enthusiasm to put together a team to bid for the record came from his admiration for the great British record-breakers who had gone before. Truly, they were all great British motorists, risking their lives to push back the barriers, and in so doing, taking lubrication,

engine and tyre technology ahead by leaps and bounds.

One of the interesting developments of the Thirties was the way that women came to take an increasingly important role as motorists. Mrs Wisdom, who raced at Brooklands and Le Mans, was by no means the only woman racing driver. Kitty Brunell also won admiration for the way she drove her MG and tuned it herself. Two great troupers of the music hall and early radio comedy, 'Gert and Daisy', alias Elsie and Doris Waters, (sisters of Jack Warner, later Sergeant Dixon of Dock Green) thought nothing of buying a Speed Six Bentley, with touring bodywork by Vanden Plas, for a continental motoring tour. Complete with goggles and helmets, they posed with the car for photographers before setting off for Dover! But it was Mrs Wisdom with her husband and the Hon. Brian Lewis, later Lord Essendon, who undertook one of the lesser-known, but thoroughly admirable, motoring feats of the 1930s.

In 1937, the Wolseley Motor company, part of the Nuffield Group, were about to launch a new 12 horsepower model. Nowadays, the motoring press are often invited to try a car out at an exotic foreign location, put up at expensive hotels, encouraged to drive the car, and fed a variety of PR handout stories proclaiming its virtues. However, the then general manager of the Wolseley company, Mr Miles Thomas, had different views. He invited Mr and Mrs Wisdom to take the new car and drive it to Baghdad! A fine test for a new British car, designed to be sold to thousands of British motorists, few of whom would ever take it out of the United Kingdom! Mr Thomas had vision, as one might expect from a man who had enlisted as a private in the Great War, served with one of the armoured car squadrons my father had helped create, and then won a commission and a Distinguished Flying Cross with the Royal Flying Corps in Egypt, before entering the car industry via journalism and promotion. Subsequently he was raised to the peerage as Lord Thomas of Remenham.

The Wisdoms duly set off, with Mr Brian Lewis in the back seat — a useful co-driver as he had considerable racing experience, including a gallant third place in the Le Mans race of 1930. They

Kitty Brunell, 1930s racing driver, fettles her MG Magna prior to a race. By the look of it Kitty is adjusting one of the SU carburettors.

crossed the Channel between Newhaven and Dieppe, powered down to Marseilles, beating the train in the process, and boarded another ferry to Tunis. From there it was straight across the desert, with Mrs Wisdom in her 'hobble' skirt, digging the car out of innumerable sand-drifts. Sand poured in through every gap and slit in the Wolseley. Arabs and Bedouins stood amazed as the little black car drove steadily by. They passed through Tripoli, across the Libyan desert to Sirte, though Italian colonial guardposts and customs barriers, bargaining for petrol and water. The sump of the engine split, they patched it up with plasticine, and so on to Benghazi, Tobruk, Mersa Matruh, Alexandria, Cairo, Jerusalem, Rutbah, Ramedi and finally to Baghdad. It must have been

a gruelling journey; years later, Tommy Wisdom recalled bathing their feet in eau-de-cologne, sensibly brought along by his wife, because they simply did not have enough supplies of water to wash in!

It was now becoming much more common for motorists to venture abroad. Captain Townsend had started his ferry boat service across the Channel in the Twenties, and though there were always problems with Customs, more and more British motorists were taking advantage of the service to use their cars for motoring holidays abroad. It brought problems to the most famous name in British car making. Rolls-Royce were obliged to warn Bentley owners that sustained high-speed cruising on the new German autobahns was likely to do damage to the engines of their cars. Indeed, Rolls-Royce brought in their new 4¼-litre overdrive Bentley saloons to counter this

A Ford Y saloon after a crash in the mid-1930s. Road accident statistics had never been worse and only improved with the introduction of the driving test and stricter speed limits in towns.

very problem. At home there were no roads like the ones in Germany and Italy, where the autobahns and autostradas were being opened up at a tremendous rate. In the Thirties, a huge international conference decided on signposting for Europe. They intended to make sure the main routes across the Continent were properly marked to help the safe passage of freight across countries. Route Number One was intended to run from London to Istanbul. Most countries did their best to make sure the road was brought up to the highest possible quality, but even in the 1980s, parts of it are not complete. Britain and France for many years could not see why it might be necessary to improve the roads from London to Dover, or from Calais to Paris, and even in 1986, the last few miles of autoroute into Calais from Paris had not been completed.

In fairness to the administrators of the time, they did try to improve roads in one or two parts of the country. In the 1920s, the Great West Road was opened, though in reality it was little more than a by-pass around Brentford, and in the 1930s, Britain suddenly decided to start building arterial roads between main centres. It was all part of a huge reaction to the number of road deaths that were occurring each year, but as with so much of inter-war policy, it was done half-heartedly, and almost too late. The Germans had not built their autobahns just for peaceful purposes, and when war came, they were much better than Britain in moving road transport of troops and armaments.

The new arterial roads looked very grand when described in newspapers and when debated at Westminster, but with hindsight, one can see how inadequate they were. My father, back in the Twenties, had argued for a major motorway system, isolated from the countryside, and raising the quality of people's lives, rather than ruining them. Motorways would take traffic away from centres of population, not right through the middle of them, and would be partially built by private

The Kingston by-pass in 1938; hailed then as one of Britain's great new roads. It was not wide enough nor built sufficiently strongly to withstand the later demands that would be made on it.

enterprise, instead of being a burden on the taxpayer.

The arterial road system was expensive with no room for expansion. Indeed, developers were allowed to build houses right next to the new main roads, subjecting future generations to a bombardment of noise and pollution. Take the Kingston by-pass, completed in 1938 with houses built either side. It all looked very fine and neat, with cars travelling gently along, cyclists able to ride side by side, and the front gardens of the new homes neat and tidy. Those same houses are there today, and they look very sad. Double-glazing is a necessity; each morning and evening traffic roars past, now hemmed in by armco barriers, with the side roads fenced off. Had my father's plans for motorway construction and design been heeded, many people nowadays would perhaps have a much higher quality of life. In the Eighties the Kingston by-pass is stretched to its limits, providing a main route in and out of London to the south-west.

Parliament was, however, trying. There had been a huge explosion of motoring in the Twenties, and the growth was continuing. Between 1930 and 1935, car production in the UK more than doubled, and around a million new cars were registered in Britain between 1933 and 1936. At this time, there was no driving test, no pedestrian crossings, and no proper system of speed limits. The result was horrific: the number of road deaths and injuries substantially increased each year. Something had to be done — and it was. In 1934, a Road Traffic Act was passed imposing a 30 miles per hour speed limit in built-up areas. Driving tests were to be brought in, and so too were pedestrian crossings. The fatality figures began to fall.

At this point, praise must be given to one Parliamentarian who did more than most to save life during his time in office, and whose work was carried on long after his death. Leslie Hore-Belisha became Minister of Transport in 1934, as a

The Motorist Defence League harangues passers-by in Hyde Park, demanding the sacking of Leslie Hore-Belisha, Minister of Transport. Belisha stayed and made valuable contributions to road safety.

absolutely vital, and Belisha beacons entered the language. Children were taught that crossings and Belisha beacons were safe, and road safety drill was brought in at many schools, with model beacons used as educational aids. Leslie Hore-Belisha was offered a seat in the Cabinet, and went on to become Secretary of State for War as Britain prepared for the forthcoming conflict. In 1954 he was given a seat in the House of Lords. Today, Belisha beacons are tending to disappear in many towns, forced out by the pressure of traffic and driver aggression, to be replaced by pelican crossings and special crossings with traffic lights. Nevertheless, the sight of children rushing out to play with their model beacons was a sign of things to come. The British have tried to take road safety seriously ever since. In 1986, declared European Road Safety Year by the EEC, Britain took a leading role, and our safety record is amongst the best in the European Community.

While many authorities were installing their new Belisha beacons, they were also trying to do something about traffic flow. It was realised that although policemen were thoroughly capable of keeping traffic moving when they were on duty at junctions, traffic lights could do the job just about as well, 24 hours a day, and cost a lot less to run, once the initial outlay had been recouped. In the Thirties, the installation of traffic light schemes became quite common, though still an event of such civic magnitude in Smethwick, for example, as to call for the Mayor himself to perform the official switching-on ceremony. The early traffic lights worked on a timing apparatus, which was normally enough to keep the flow going well. After the war, various systems were tried to make traffic lights responsive to changes in traffic loads. Pneumatic pads were used for many years, giving way to electronic sensor cables buried in the road surface. Today, traffic lights in most urban areas are linked to a central computer. In London, the computer is linked to Scotland Yard. Highly experienced traffic police can adjust the flow to suit local conditions in a wide area of the capital, using television cameras perched on high buildings or on lamp standards, and able to be moved and focused from a control desk by the policeman on duty. Only recently, a

member of the National Government. He put into effect the new pedestrian crossings (though the 'zebra' stripes did not appear till 1957), with amber flashing lights known as 'Belisha beacons' on either side. They caused an outcry; drivers were obliged to stop at a crossing if anyone was walking across, or about to walk across. The Motorist Defence League sprang into being, calling for Mr Hore-Belisha to be sacked and claiming these silly crossings and their flashing lamps were unnecessary. They were, of course,

desperately sick child was rushed from South Mimms in Hertfordshire all the way to the Westminster Children's Hospital for an emergency operation at the height of the London rush-hour. The ambulance made the journey in less than half an hour, with the senior collator in the traffic division advising his colleagues on the ground, and in panda cars, which section of road to clear ahead, and with the computer being used to adjust the traffic lights in front. Motorists were warned of the hold-up and, more importantly, the reason why, by close liaison with the London radio stations. Traffic control has moved on a great deal from the days of the early traffic lights and Belisha beacons.

Another great safety measure brought in during the Thirties was the cats-eye. It seems such a simple idea now, yet when originally patented it was a major breakthrough. The cats-eye reflected back the lights from headlamps as a car sped forward along the road, providing the driver with an accurate guide of which way the road was

Children carrying out to the school playing-field the model Belisha beacons which were used to instruct them in the new road safety drill.

going. The cats-eye sat in its own rubber holder set into the road. If a car ran over the cats-eye, the device sank down into the holder, wiping its optical parts on a ridge of rubber as it did so, causing them to be cleaned. It was and is a simple concept, but one which many other countries have still to adopt.

There were a number of other important safety moves during the Thirties; a new Highway Code was published, the Trunk Roads Act was brought in to give the Minister of Transport responsibility for the main road system, and new lighting restrictions were brought in to reduce dazzle at night. At the same time, the cumbersomely-named but vital Restriction of Ribbon Development Act was taken through Parliament, ending house construction along certain sections of road. It could not remove, however, the homes that had already been built alongside the new main roads.

95

▲Civic pride in West Bromwich as Mr Mayor switches on a new traffic light system, bringing some order out of traffic chaos in the borough.

The huge explosion in car ownership provided plenty of jobs in the car plants, though these were often uncertain. Workers might be hired for several months, then laid off as demand dropped. Much of the work was on piece-rates; a lathe operator might make so many widgets in a shift, but the more he made, the more money he got. Those two approaches were to cause enormous problems for the car industry in the years ahead; the casual nature of employment led to mass trade-union membership and then confrontation, and the piece-rate system encouraged quantity rather than quality production.

The motor car's popularity caused two events at the end of the decade: the first, the Motor Show, which had been held at Olympia under the patronage of His Majesty the King, was switched to Earl's Court and the new exhibition halls. It would make Earl's Court its home until the late 1970s. The second, more serious perhaps, especially in view of the way many of its warnings went ignored, was the Bressey Report on London's traffic problems. Successive governments have fudged or ignored the crisis and in the

Eighties, London is choking under the motor vehicle.

For the mass market, it was Ford that took over the running once more in the 1930s. Morris and Austin might have had it all, or nearly all, their own way in the late Twenties, but the Ford investment at Dagenham and the giant plant there was bound to pay dividends. The Ford Y model, followed by the Ford Popular of 1937, put Ford very much ahead of its rivals, especially when in 1935, at a special Ford exhibition at the Albert Hall, it was announced that the company had slashed its price for the Model Y to just £100. Within months, two out of every five 8

◄ 1931 — miseries of an English picnic! The three picnicers, despite their furs, seem on the verge of frostbite and not even the prospect of the journey home in their new Triumph Scorpion can raise their spirits.

▲ Two seaside revellers practice skiing along the beach behind the latest four-door Ford Prefect in the last summer before the war. This 1939 car was the shape of things to come in the post-war years.

horsepower or under cars sold in Britain were Fords, and the company had 22 per cent of the UK car market. The Popular, brought in shortly afterwards, kept Ford well ahead of the rest.

It is well worth comparing the 1931 Triumph Scorpion, with its running boards, two doors and cramped bodywork, to the four-door Ford Prefect of 1939 towing the sand-skiers along the beach. The Prefect has a unitary construction, solid pressed-steel wheels and features we would think of as modern. It was the shape of things to come, once the world had fought another war. Motorists too would change in style, as the masses realised that driving was theirs, too, for the taking.

War came to Europe for the second time in 21 years when the German tanks rolled over the Polish border on 1 September 1939. The House of Commons met the next day, and on the Sunday morning of 3 September at 11.00 BBC announcer Alvar Liddell introduced Prime Minister Neville Chamberlain at the microphone. Chamberlain told the nation that despite warnings, German troops were continuing their invasion of Poland and that Britain was therefore at war with Germany.

On many levels it would be a very different war from the one fought in 1914-18. For a start, it would involve more nations fighting in more theatres of war. It would not be a war just between soldiers, sailors and airmen; this time whole civilian populations would bear the brunt too. And although the horrors of the trench warfare of the Western Front would be avoided, massacres of civilians and prisoners of war, the murder of the Jews and the appalling terror of the first atomic bombs would make the Second World War as horrifying as the First.

Like the First War, too, the consequences of the 1939-45 conflict for the motor vehicle would be momentous. When the troops of the Kaiser, the Tsar, the King-Emperor and the République Française went to war in 1914, they went by railway. Motor vehicles were in their infancy from a military point of view, best used for personal transport for senior officers, and perhaps as ambulances and field tenders. By 1918, it was realised that the motor vehicle was an essential arm of war, just as those spindly, rickety aircraft of 1914 had become part of modern battle.

By 1939, Britain was still not ready to wage a modern war in Europe. Years of neglect in the Twenties and early Thirties could not be put right overnight. The Royal Navy, Britain's pride, consisted largely of ships and cruisers dating from the era of Jutland. The Royal Air Force had but

◀Better news for the allies: the Prime Minister poses for his cheering troops at the Victory Parade in Tunis in 1941. Though the photograph is signed by Field Marshal Earl Alexander of Tunis, the man sitting behind Monty is in fact General Sir Oliver Leese.

recently abandoned its bi-plane fighters in favour of the new Spitfires and Hurricanes, and indeed the Fleet Air Arm went to war and helped sink the Bismarck using ancient Fairey Swordfish torpedo bombers, still with bi-plane wings, held together with wire and known affectionately to their crews as 'Stringbags'. The Army was also very much unprepared. The country which, thanks to Mr Churchill's energy, had brought tanks into modern war and used them with stunning effect at the Battle of Cambrai, had more or less tried to forget about the tank once peace had come. The cavalry regiments, most natural candidates to use the new weapons, had stayed loyal to their horses, which had served General Allenby so well in his march on Jerusalem. Indeed, those same cavalry regiments had in 1939 only recently been mechanised, with tanks that were not the equal of those being used by the new Wehrmacht. There were similar problems in the motor transport field. The RAF had only recently given up using lorries with solid tyres, which shook apart everyone and everything that travelled inside. Modern scout cars did not exist. This lack of foresight was not a formula for success, and had the modern designs existed, and the factories to build them, the lack of an even halfway decent road system would have caused all sorts of problems getting the new equipment to a new army in being. There again, there was no new army.

But Britain pinned her faith in their alliance with the French. There was no Marshal Foch to lead to battle the combined armies, but the French did have a magnificent line of defensive forts, linked by underground tunnels and railways, and called the Maginot Line. Let the Germans come and throw themselves in vain on the battlements and fortifications. The French were dug in, and the Germans could do their worst. Unfortunately the Germans were quite good at that. In 1939 Hitler concluded a non-aggression pact with the Russians, and was quite careful not to commit himself to fighting on two fronts. So while he mopped up Poland, smashing its brave but hopelessly under-strength and under-equipped armed forces, he did nothing in the West. It was the era of the 'phoney war'. The notes of the Polish National Anthem went silent on Radio

Warsaw and Hitler was free to strike on France. The French High Command braced itself behind the Maginot Line and the men and officers of the British Expeditionary Force prepared for battle. At this point, Hitler changed the rules. Instead of hurling his men on the redoubts of the Maginot Line, he used his fast-moving armoured columns and mechanised battalions to go right round it. France had not extended the Maginot Line to cover the Franco-Belgian border — it would not have been very diplomatic to their Belgian friends and allies — so no Maginot Line, a hopelessly inadequate Belgian army, and the Germans poured straight through.

This time there was to be no 'Miracle of the Marne' and no 'Angel of Mons'. The French army collapsed under the German Blitzkrieg, helped by a patent lack of morale and political will and a strategy founded on defence and the horrors of Verdun. The British fell back on the Channel ports, losing most of their equipment, such as it was. There were moments of great gallantry. Major Tony Rolt, who would in the next decade become one of Britain's great racing drivers and who would win Le Mans in Coronation year, distinguished himself in the defence of Calais. But when the little ships came over to Dunkirk to take from the beaches the remnants of Britain's army, there was no doubt that this country had suffered a massive defeat; the best of her professional army beaten, its equipment scattered. The Royal Air Force had suffered too; it had lost planes, men, ground crew and spares in the long fallback to the Channel, and though the Navy made Dunkirk possible and was still in being, it had world-wide commitments. There was ample reason for despair in Britain in 1940.

At home, motoring had all but stopped on 3 September 1939, with the declaration of war with petrol rationing and blackout imposed. Drivers had little fuel to spare for private motoring and there was a basic ration for all cars which meant in practice that the average driver got a ration of 150 miles a month. It was difficult to buy a foreign car either; on the day war broke out, the Government banned the import of cars from abroad. In fact a number of deliveries arrived; some Hudsons came in as late as the spring of 1940.

An advertisement for one of the officially permitted masks used to cover headlamps during the wartime blackout. It was claimed you could drive with safety, but road accidents increased, despite petrol rationing.

late as the spring of 1940.

On the other hand, there was plenty of damage done with the cars that remained, even on the tiny amounts of fuel permitted. The blackout brought an explosion of road accidents; more people died on the roads on Britain between August and Christmas 1939 than were killed in active service. The headlight masks approved by the Government allowed just a glimmer of light onto the roads. Pedestrians, cyclists and other drivers were at terrible risk, and though in February 1940 a night-

A far cry from the royal limousines: the Daimler scout car, airborne during action. Several of these useful and gallant little vehicles still survive and turn out regularly at Daimler-Lanchester owners' club meetings.

time speed limit of 20 miles per hour was imposed, the accidents continued. It was not until 1942, with the abolition of the basic petrol ration, that the accident statistics eased.

Many experiments were tried to get round the petrol restrictions; the car with a gasbag on top made a reappearance, but it was not satisfactory. There were problems with supplies and the cars tended to misfire. In the country, where people were allowed enough petrol for two shopping trips and one visit to Church each week, experiments were also carried out using methane gas obtained from chicken manure, and wood-burning stoves to generate gas. They were not remarkably successful either. Even with enough petrol to drive, the next problem was where to drive to. Vast areas of the country suddenly became prohibited war zones. Night-time motorists were apt to run into enthusiastic members of the Home Guard, convinced that each car might contain hand-picked members of Hitler's SS, disguised as

nuns. By day, it was little better. Convinced that the enemy was poised to invade, the authorities had encouraged the removal of signposts from junctions. Drivers did not know which way to turn, and it was not much good trying to look routes up on the map. Maps and guides had suddenly assumed a military significance and disappeared from the shops. There was no doubt the British wanted to make sure their rolling and confusing English roads played their part in the defence of the nation.

Motorists were encouraged by the authorities to make sure their cars were locked away at all times, and immobilised. Had the Germans arrived, and forced their way into the garages of the homes of Dover, Folkestone, Bexhill and Hastings, they would have found hundreds of cars minus their rotor arms! Quite a few motorists must have improved their knowledge of the mechanics of a car as a result of this Government measure. Others had to find out more, just to keep their cars running, for skilled motor mechanics were suddenly in demand by the Armed Forces.

As planned by special secret committees set up by Lord Nuffield, many car plants in Britain went over to military production within a few days of the outbreak of war. There was to be little call for the giant Daimler limousines which had provided transport for King George VI and his family. Instead the Armed Forces had a desperate need for a tough little armoured car for reconnaissance purposes. The result was the Daimler Scout Car, sometimes called the Dingo, an immensely rugged machine, where the driver sat almost sideways on, and had a choice of five gears forward or backwards. It was especially useful in the Western desert, and in the fighting in Europe after D-Day.

The Vauxhall company made a remarkable contribution to the war effort, designing and putting into production Britain's first major battle tank, the Churchill, in just one year. The Churchill weighed 38 tons, and could be adapted to a number of different roles. When the Allied Forces invaded Normandy in 1944, there were bridge-laying Churchills, flame-throwing Churchills, ones fitting with flailing chains at the front to clear minefields, even versions designed to work in the surf. It was

Road testing the latest Vauxhall! This is a
Churchill tank designed and put into production in
just one year; it subsequently distinguished itself
on all war fronts.

an outstanding achievement by the company, using all the same sort of skills which were needed to make cars and heavy lorries, and applying them to the war effort.

All car firms were caught up in the drive to make the machinery of war. While Vauxhall was making the Churchill tank and turning out hundreds of Bedford lorries, the giant Ford plant at Dagenham was being camouflaged with the aid of experts from the Air Ministry. It was painted from above so as to resemble a giant area of marshland, which was exactly what it had been before the plant was built. Inside, all kinds of machinery were being built on the huge assembly lines; tractors to help plough the new areas of virgin farmland needed to help the country feed itself; bren gun carriers, extraordinarily complicated tracked vehicles used to carry machine guns into action; vast numbers of lorries, some with four-wheel drive.

The mass-production techniques in which Ford specialised were employed elsewhere too. Rolls-Royce and Bentley cars had gone out of production almost as soon as war had been declared — there was little need for that sort of car in this sort of war. Besides, Ernest Hives, the Rolls-Royce chief, and his designers and engineers had more important work to do. The great company had developed the Merlin aero-engine, the power behind the Spitfire and Hurricane. Suddenly huge numbers of Merlin engines were needed, not just for the two fighter planes, but for all the other aircraft which could use them. Lancaster and Mosquito bombers and American P-51 Mustangs were just three of the other aircraft types which would use the Merlin before the war ended, and it was vital for Rolls-Royce to learn the tricks and techniques of mass production in a few months. There was no company better to turn to for help than Ford.

Before the war, a lot of work had been done on dispersing factory facilities. It was no good concentrating all machinery and workers in one place if that vital factory was bombed, so in the months after Munich, vast numbers of 'shadow' factories were planned. Once war had been declared, these shadow plants came into operation, making aircraft, lorries, engines and tanks. The

most famous, and the most successful perhaps, was at Urmston in Manchester where Rolls-Royce and Ford co-operated to make Merlin engines. They took on workers who knew little or nothing about mechanics, let alone aero-engine manufacture, and yet by the time the war ended, the Urmston plant was employing over 17,000 staff, and had made over 34,000 Merlin engines for the RAF, not one of which was ever rejected.

Once the United States entered the war, the supply of vehicles increased still further. Notable among these was the jeep. Vast numbers of people were needed to drive them and here women came into their own, as they had done in the First World War. Women could drive trucks and tenders and deliver stores to bases and airfields. They also made first-class chauffeurs for senior officers, freeing men for the Forces. Perhaps there is no more telling picture of the shape of the Second World War than the shot of the Princess Elizabeth as a junior ATS officer doing her course in motor maintenance.

Two of the great motorists of the war were British: Prime Minister Winston Churchill and Field Marshal Montgomery. Churchill knew the value of being seen by British troops, and realised a lot more troops could see a lot more of him if he inspected them from the back of a car. So when he came to Tunis in 1941 for the Victory Parade, Churchill was driven past his troops in the back of 'Old Faithful', Monty's open-top Humber staff car. Monty himself kept a whole convoy of personal vehicles with him throughout the war. He lived in a series of caravans with his personal staff around him at all times. It made for efficiency in waging war, and efficiency was precisely what Montgomery demanded at all times.

While the war was going on, the car maker's minds were far from idle. They knew that cars would be needed when peace finally arrived, and that the motor industry would be vital as Britain attempted to rebuild its shattered fortunes. The

▶Girls of the ATS Motor Transport section leap into their vehicles in 1942, revealing many a shapely leg! Thousands of women joined the forces, including HRH Princess Elizabeth, and they made a vital contribution to the war effort.

Touring through Melbourne in 1947, Field Marshal Montgomery in his stately Humber.

Jaguar plant in Coventry was given over to the war effort, but senior staff on the roof watching for fires during the bombings occupied their spare moments by trying to design the car they wanted to build once hostilities had ended. The result for William Lyons and his team was the Jaguar XK120. It went on show at the Motor Show at Earl's Court in 1948 and was quite literally a 'show-stopper'. It had long, slinky lines that spoke speed and excitement to the crowds. Asked why he had chosen the figure 120, Lyons explained that was because the new Jaguar Sports was capable of 120 miles per hour. He was greeted by disbelief. The following spring, Lyons took a group of journalists to a piece of newly-completed motorway at Jabbeke in Belgium. He had the motorway closed off, and one of the new XK120s driven along it at speed. 120 miles per hour? The car did the 'flying mile' at over 132! It made a

sensation overnight, and Lyons was well on his way to becoming the most significant figure in Britain's post-war motor industry.

More prosaic was the new car dreamt up by a brilliant designer at Morris, Alec Issigonis. He knew there was a need for a first-class utilitarian saloon car, and in 1948 he exhibited the Morris Minor. It was bulbous and rather fussy in one or two respects, but it was exactly what the country wanted, and it stayed in production for years. Economical, which was vital for a country still being rationed, the Minor was the first of a whole series of post-war British family cars which brought motoring finally to the masses. And that is where the next part of the story begins.

132·6 M.P.H. ON PUMP PETROL

On May 30th, 1949, an entirely standard Jaguar 3½ litre XK 120 Sports Two-Seater, running on pump fuel, attained a speed of 132.6 m.p.h. over a flying mile on the Jabbeke-Aeltre Road in Belgium. This speed was officially timed by the Royal Automobile Club of Belgium and is the fastest ever recorded by a standard production unsupercharged car.

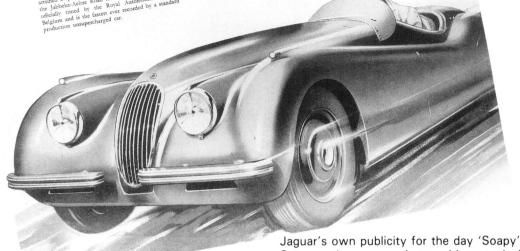

Jaguar's own publicity for the day 'Soapy' Soames, the company's test driver, took the new XK 120 Jaguar to over 132 miles per hour on a bit of Belgian motorway.

Alec Issigonis's first great masterpiece of automotive design: the new Morris Minor, launched at the Motor Show at Earl's Court in 1948. Note the low slung headlamps and split windscreen.

Supreme in Economy

The new **MORRIS MINOR** makes the most of your petrol. goes farther on a tankful. Traditional Morris reliability and low maintenance are inherent in this modern design.

In 1958 the Prime Minister, Mr Harold Macmillan, was attributed with the remark, 'You've never had it so good'. It was an observation which at the time earned 'Supermac' quite a few smiles, was later used as an example of British arrogance and complacency, but which with the passage of time has become grudgingly acknowledged as accurate. The British spent the Fifties trying to rebuild after the years of shattering war, and though they could not achieve the economic miracle of Germany, by 1960, Britain had its highest standard of living ever.

In no other area was this more obvious than motoring and the British motorist. Motoring in Britain had expanded in the inter-war years and after the Second World War, it exploded. In 1955, new car registrations topped the half-million mark for the first time; in 1960 over 800,000 new cars were licensed. It meant vast numbers of new drivers coming onto the roads and thousands of jobs in the reborn British motor industry. There would be a time during the Fifties when the UK motor and motorcycle industry was the world's second largest, and though the British car industry never achieved America's enormous output, the strength of the UK car makers was enough to exert considerable political and economic leverage on the fortunes of the country. At one point, indeed, the Minister of Transport seemed almost as important as the Chancellor of the Exchequer!

It was an era of enormous change, and not just in Britain. Internationally, the balance of world power had changed irrevocably. Britain and her Empire were diminished as a superpower; though still strong economically and militarily, Britain could not hope to stand alone, nor could any of the European powers. The world was split between East and West: on one side stood Russia and her allies, willing and unwilling; on the other stood America and her friends. Nominally, it was a time of peace — in fact it was more of an armed truce, with a ceasefire which kept breaking down. Throughout the Fifties, both sides would make trial of one another's strength, beginning with the

siege of Berlin and the airlift at the end of the Forties, then the Korean war and culminating in the showdown of the Cuban missiles crisis in 1962.

Colonial empires were swept away either by force, as with the French in Indo-China, or peacefully, as with the British. In new capitals around the world, the Union Jack was lowered at many Independence ceremonies. British Royals jetted across the world to smile sweetly, to wish the new country well, and to cheer the departing planters, farmers, engineers, administrators and civil servants who had made and run these parts of the Empire. There were still plenty of jobs and plenty of economic opportunities in the new Commonwealth countries for the British, but it would never be quite the same again. A wind of change, as Mr Macmillan said, had swept over Africa, but it had equally swept over the British and their island kingdom.

At home, war-time conditions persisted. Rationing lasted well into the Fifties, and there were all sorts of restrictions on motoring. It was the era of National Service, dried egg powder and Ealing Comedies.

Great changes, though, were afoot: the effects of the Education Act of 1944 were being felt; the Beveridge Report was being translated into the welfare state; and most important of all, the National Health Service was brought into being. Steel and coal were being nationalised as Mr Attlee's administration pushed through the most ambitious programme of social, economic and national reform ever mounted by a British government. Clement Attlee, with his pipe and moustache, epitomised the little Briton, getting life back to normal. And then there was Cripps. Labour's new Chancellor, Sir Stafford Cripps, was probably the most austere man ever to grace British politics. He lived, according to his enemies, on a diet consisting mainly of white of egg, and was a sick man even when Labour came to power. His slogan to British industry was direct: Export or bust, he told them, and that was exactly what the British motor industry set out to do, amid some of the biggest supply and cash-flow problems ever known. Cars went for export, for foreign earnings. Cars in Britain in the early Fifties were

◀The M1 finally under construction in the 1950s. My father advocated the road in the early 1920s!

on quotas and you had to fight to get one. Once the cash had been found to buy the car, all sorts of further problems loomed; there was swingeing taxation and difficulties with parts.

While Labour was forcing through its policies at the end of the war and into the Fifties, Britain was growing. There was a huge boom in the population over the ten years between 1941 and 1951, from 45 to 50 million people — a giant leap for a nation at war or on its economic beam ends. There would be a further leap of six million over the following 20 years, but there was nothing to compare with the sudden post-war baby boom. Families were young and they were growing, and they wanted the luxuries they felt they had earned, and which they saw in American homes on their visits to the cinema. In short, there was a growing consumer demand, and once it was unleashed, Britain would know nothing quite like it.

But in the early Fifties, because of the quota restrictions or the demands of the export effort, it was hard to get that coveted car. Either families

This 1950s beauty in her fur-trimmed coat looks on admiringly as the man from the BSM shows her how easy it is to adjust the Wolseley's engine! Sexist it may have been but women were becoming motorists in increasing numbers.

went without, or they tried to use a pre-war car. It was possible to order a car in 1948 and not be offered delivery until 1954. The British Motor Trade Association set up a scheme to try to prevent a black market: they would not take in a car for resale for a year after delivery, and this was later extended to two years. It was a scheme still in force for cars like the Jaguar in Coronation year. Cars cost more, too. Purchase tax had been brought in during the war, adding hugely to the price of motoring, but with no-one in the war years buying a car, few people had noticed. Now it was there and the days of the cheap car had gone. At the top end of the market, the Government decided to put on double purchase tax for any car which cost over a thousand pounds. This put pressure

In a desperate attempt to imbue its latest version of the Minx saloon with some sort of appeal to the man in the street, Hillman gave the Minx a new slogan and used a model to pose beside it, apparently struggling to open the door.

on the car makers to produce cars for less, and led many of the smaller firms into difficulties. In fact, during the early Fifties, the purchase tax rate was continually used as a regulator as the experts at the Treasury sought to get the economy on to an even keel.

There were a lot of car firms in production: Allard, Austin, Jaguar, Daimler, Lea-Francis, Alvis, Hillman, Bentley, Rolls-Royce, Morris, MG, Wolseley, Sunbeam, Singer, Armstrong-Siddeley, Aston Martin, Rover, Standard and Triumph were all making cars and were all British. During the decade, there would be crises and

mergers: Austin merged with Morris to become BMC; Jaguar took over Daimler; Lea-Francis gave up making cars, as would Armstrong-Siddeley in due course. Britain might be a leader in the world when it came to making cars, but in the boardrooms of the big companies it was anything but a rosy existence.

What about the motorists themselves? Thousands of people had learnt to drive during the war, though there was quite a difference betwen handling a Daimler Scout Car and a Hillman Minx or Standard Vanguard. Many of them wanted to use their new ability and experience, and so were ready to put up with just about anything the car makers wanted to offer them; purchase tax, export quotas, Motor Trade Association restrictions, whatever. For those who could not drive, an industry flourished in the shape of the driving school. Learning to drive was quite easy so long as one had the right teacher and the right tuition. The British School of Motoring, for one, grew quickly on such a policy, and was careful to use pretty models in its publicity snaps, alongside the wise and experienced driving instructor!

Two cars were thrust at the British during this period — the Hillman Minx, my first car, and the Standard Vanguard. Both had the typical slab-sided shape that the Americans had pioneered, but to today's eyes were rather ugly; on the other hand, they were solid motor cars. Sir John Black, the managing director of Standard, actually sat on the bonnet of the new model, in the heart of the Dales, to show how rugged it was, though Hillman seemed to prefer the traditional 'with model' shot when it unveiled the new 'Gay Look' Minx at the Motor Show of 1955. If in doubt, the motor manufacturers said, give a model a facelift and give the motoring writers a generous lunch, and you'll be surprised what good publicity you'll get! Despite the ugly design of both the Vanguard and the Minx, this was a time when buyers were queueing up to get what they could, and so both cars sold. In fact, the boom in the British car industry was founded on the sales of thousands of cars like these. It meant that when the crunch came, 20 years on, some British firms would still think they could get away with bad design and an arrogant 'we know best' approach towards the consumer. The consumer had other ideas, and took his custom elsewhere.

One area of car sales which the British did get right was sports cars. There was very little opposition in the world markets for the British sports car; in the immediate post-war years, the Germans, French and Italians were nowhere to be seen, and the Americans had little notion of the sort of sports car that the British could make. In fact, their customers wanted our sports and rally cars. So cars like the Jaguar XK120 and Jowett Javelin went for export, boosted by the company's good showings in motor sport. Sydney Allard had similar success with his range of sports cars, and thought nothing of entering himself in events like the Monte-Carlo rally. He won the event in 1952, expecting to come home and be acclaimed for the

hero he was. Unfortunately for him, news of his victory coincided with the announcement of the death of King George VI.

Surprisingly, some of the prettiest sports cars of the Fifties came from the same company that produced the unattractive Standard Vanguard. Standard had acquired the Triumph name and used it on a series of sports cars with the TR prefix. The original Triumph Roadster was not highly thought of, though in the Eighties its reputation lifted when used by TV detective Jim Bergerac. It was the next in the series that excited people, the low-slung TR2, and the TR3 and TR3A which followed it. These cars had, for their time, fantastic performance and handling, and were highly-praised for it when they took part in rallies and motor races.

There were several real British success stories in the Fifties, and they were not confined to mass producers securing export successes. After the war, a man called David Brown was able to gain control of both the Aston Martin and Lagonda companies. They were great names; a Lagonda had won Le Mans in 1935, and there had been a very fine third place in 1939, when W.O. Bentley, released from his contract at Rolls-Royce, had been the firm's chief engineer. Aston Martin cars had never before won Le Mans, but they had had highly-creditable class victories. Brown set out to make the Aston Martin a success, and although his involvement with tractor manufacture led to many joking comparisons between the tractors and the cars, he took Aston by the scruff of the neck and turned it into a world-beating sports car.

Prince Philip was among those who patronised the Aston Martin Lagonda; he had one of the late Fifties Lagonda Rapides, and used it to drive the Queen on many occasions. In those days it was not considered entirely necessary to carry a detective in the car. Nowadays, that lack of security would not be tolerated.

Throughout the Fifties, under a Conservative government dedicated to setting the people free, Aston Martin made efforts to win the coveted Le Mans race. It eluded them each year, despite the quality of the team — which included Stirling Moss — and the extent of their preparation. This involved taking the whole team, cars included, to the village of Chartre-sur-le-Loire, some 20 miles outside Le Mans, and taking over the Hôtel de France as race headquarters. If you go to the hotel today, you will find dozens of pictures in the bar commemorating the Le Mans race, and in particular, the Aston team of the Fifties. During some high jinks in the river nearby, Stirling Moss even lost his false teeth one year, and a new set had to be sent from England! The Aston team recreated the Bentley spirit of the Twenties, and it was entirely right and proper in 1959, with the Jaguar works team retired, that Carroll Shelby, the American ace, and Roy Salvadori should take the Aston team to what remains their sole Le Mans victory. Never was there a team that tried so hard to win, nor a team whose efforts are better remembered. Each year at the time of the Le Mans race, the Hôtel de France is packed: modern aces like Derek Bell and David Hobbs stay there, linking past and present.

But if Aston Martin and their drivers were the great triers of the Fifties, the great winners were Jaguar. It was right that William Lyons should take his company back to the Le Mans track at the start of the decade to seek to establish a legend, and he was entirely successful. Jaguar are today selling cars years later on the combination of value for money, luxury, performance and sporting heritage which Lyons set up. For the British motor sports enthusiast of the Fifties, nothing was so exciting as hearing the crackly radio reports from the trackside in north-west France as the Jaguars stamped their mark all over the Sarthe circuit. And though the Bentley victories of the Twenties still have that touch of epic quality which the Jaguar triumphs lacked, it is no shame to the Coventry firm and its drivers — the Jaguar team drivers, led by 'Lofty' England, made Le Mans their own in this era.

There were some famous drivers in the Jaguar

The Duke of Edinburgh drives the Queen back to Buckingham Palace after their holiday at Sandringham in February 1958, in a Lagonda convertible. Among the badges on the bumper are the RAC and AA, the Company of Veteran Motorists and the most coveted badge of all, the British Racing Drivers' Club — BRDC.

team: Stirling Moss, Tony Rolt, Mike Hawthorn, Duncan Hamilton, Peter Walker and Peter Whitehead, Peter Collins, Ron Flockhart, Ivor Bueb and Ninian Sanderson. All of them either won a Le Mans or were placed second. There were five Jaguar victories, three by the works team and two by the Écurie Écosse, the privateer Scottish team which had such close links with the Jaguar factory. And they took the great race to higher and higher speeds than ever before. The C and D-Type Jaguars which they drove at Le Mans were some of the greatest racing cars ever built. They were designed especially to win Le Mans, by now a billiard-table smooth racetrack, which the best cars could lap at over a hundred miles per hour. The cars were the creation of Bill Heynes, who chalked out the design for the chassis on the floor of the Jaguar development shop. The bodies were beautiful, streamlined and low, and the machine used the normal Jaguar engine, especially strengthened and reinforced, and powerfully tuned. The result was history. In 1950, Jaguar had entered a normal XK120, the next year the first C-Type was ready, and a team of three set out to win the great race.

Le Mans is rarely won without drama, and though Stirling Moss led the field after five laps, there was a problem with the Jaguar's oil feed. Vibrations broke a vital pipe, and first one, then Moss's Jaguar ground to a halt. One Jaguar was left — a racewinner if only it would keep going. Peter Whitehead and Peter Walker, two gentlemen farmers, had the drive, and they kept on with agricultural solidity to win at four o'clock on the Sunday afternoon.

The victory did wonders for Jaguar overnight, not just at home, but around the world, and the following year, William Lyons took his team racing again. This time it was a flop. Jaguar was trying the new disc brakes, and though these worked marvellously well, the company was worried about the new racing Mercedes, which seemed to have the edge on the Jaguars for top speed. Jaguar fitted new streamlined bodies, but

◀ Aston Martin's triumph at Le Mans in 1959: it was a great win for the British firm.

they affected the engine cooling, and all three cars broke down with engine problems.

1953 was much better, though due only to one of those freak chances that seem to crop up in British motor sport. Tony Rolt, ex-Army officer, and Duncan Hamilton, ex-fighter pilot, had been disqualified for some minor infringement in practice. Not unnaturally, they went out to get as drunk as they could, only for William Lyons to find them with the news that the disqualification had been lifted, and they had better sober up. Moss went out in the lead Jaguar, but soon came back in with fuel supply problems. Then Rolt and Hamilton did their bit; they drove like angels to win the race for Jaguar and Britain, and in so doing made disc brakes acceptable to motor manufacturers all over the world. It was a great victory for Coronation year.

The next year saw the new D-Type Jaguar, even more streamlined and fitted with a great fin, probably the most beautiful sports racing car ever made. The 1954 trip to Le Mans was unsuccessful, the Jaguars only managing second to Ferrari, but in 1955 came another victory with Hawthorn and Ivor Bueb taking first place. Their glory was spoiled by accusations that Hawthorn had been to blame for the dreadful crash in which Pierre Levegh's Mercedes had shot off the track into the crowd, killing many spectators, but it was a victory all the same. Some time later, Hawthorn was cleared by the authorities.

While the works team was doing so well the Écurie Écosse was starting to do even better. In 1956, when the works team hit trouble, the Écurie drivers, Ron Flockhart and Ninian Sanderson, went on to win. The next year, Flockhart, this time partnered by Bueb, did it again, with Sanderson, this time partnered by Jock Lawrence, in second place, and a French D-Type private entry in third. It was supreme Jaguar dominance in the 24-hour race, with five triumphs to match the Bentley achievement, and it had made the reputation of the firm famous right around the world. By 1959, Jaguars were not competitive and David Brown's Aston Martin team duly recorded a well-deserved victory at the Le Mans track. It is important to realise that the British achievement at Le Mans is greater than any other nation. British cars have

While Britons battled gamely in the racing world our designers were not idle either. This is the Vanguard, for which production began in 1948 for the export market only. On the bonnet is Sir John Black, the company's managing director, who clearly believed in selling the product himself!

won the race more times than cars from any other country: British drivers more times than drivers from any other nation.

Today, drivers like Derek Bell maintain the British tradition. Bell has now won the race four times, which puts him ahead of all other Britons, though he has yet to equal Woolf Barnato's triumph of winning a hat-trick of victories. In recent years, Aston Martin and Jaguar have started to return to Le Mans to challenge the present Porsche dominance. But in the Fifties it was the story of the Twenties all over again: British cars and British drivers sweeping the board in the great 24-hour race. However, Le Mans was not the only

motor race worth winning anymore. Motor racing had moved on.

Four young Britons were making world-wide reputations in a somewhat different sphere of racing. The Grand Prix circus, as we understand it today, did not get going until 1950. There had been Grand Prix races in various countries before this: the French Grand Prix, for example, dated back to 1906, when Renault were triumphant, and in the Thirties, the Mercedes and Auto-Union teams had battled for supremacy against the Italian Alfa-Romeo team across a series of national Grand Prix events. But it was only in 1950 that the system came to be applied across Grand Prix racing. It

Golden boy Mike Hawthorn, Britain's first world motor racing champion, with the Vanwall and mechanics at Silverstone in May 1955. Note how smart and tidy the mechanics are and Hawthorn's eternal bow tie which he always wore when racing.

119

meant that there could be a world champion driver, and at once the focus of motor racing changed for ever.

The four young Britons were Tony Brooks, Peter Collins, Mike Hawthorn and Stirling Moss, and they are remembered in ascending order: Collins was killed motor-racing; Hawthorn died at the wheel of his Jaguar on the Guildford by-pass a few months after winning the World Championship; Brooks drove a British car to its first Grand Prix victory for 32 years; while Moss became the most famous British racing driver for a generation without ever winning a championship. All had or have great virtues, both as drivers and as men, and all four were British motorists of the most outstanding merit.

Moss and Hawthorn were the oldest of the four and they were quickly into action in the post-war years. In 1948, Moss won a number of races in the then Formula Three series, and went on to win the famous Tourist Trophy race in 1950 at the wheel of a Jaguar. He was then just 20 years old. Nowadays, the great Formula One teams would have been queueing up, vying for his services, but in the early days there was not the organisation, the sponsors or the money. So Moss drove a number of rather uncompetitive British racing cars, raced for the Jaguar team at Le Mans, broke records with a Jaguar at the great banked racetrack at Montlhery outside Paris, and waited. He was offered a drive by Ferrari at a Grand Prix at Bari, but when he got there, someone else got the drive, and Moss went on his way, vowing never to drive for Ferrari. He didn't — something Ferrari himself would later describe as 'my biggest mistake'. Moss was a very dedicated young man who took racing seriously. He was not the hard-living, hard-drinking, man-about-town playboy racer that one would have found in the Bentley teams. Early to bed, early to rise and do the job properly was the Moss philosophy, and in the Fifties, that was something rather new.

Mike Hawthorn was much more the playboy. He was the embodiment of the dashing

Jaguars one and two at Le Mans in 1957, recreating a double British victory at almost exactly the same point that Bentleys did in 1929.

121

Englishman, with a mop of fair hair brushed back in the best Brylcreem manner, whereas what hair the young Stirling had was thinning fast. Mike Hawthorn always wore a bow-tie when he drove, and when he drove, he drove very fast indeed. While Moss was looking around for a competitive drive, Hawthorn joined Ferrari and managed a third place in the 1954 Drivers' Championship. Moss, though, had not been idle. Despairing of getting a manufacturer to take him on as a works driver, he had bought his own Maserati, and prepared and entered it with such good effect that Maserati gave him help and assistance. Then in 1955, he was taken on by the Mercedes team as number two to their great driver Juan Manuel Fangio. That season, Fangio won the Drivers' Championship, with Moss as runner-up. Mercedes was dominating post-war racing as it had done before the war.

And runner-up was what Moss was fated to be for the rest of his racing career. He became the most famous British racing driver of the decade, though he never won a Le Mans 24-hour race and was never world motor racing champion. In fact he was second in the Drivers' Championship for four years on the trot, and third for the three years after that. He was twice second-placed in the Le Mans race, though he led it several times, and was always first away from the grid at the famous Le Mans start. The British have produced dozens of first-class drivers, and many champions, but Moss has a special place in the pantheon, as the great racer who never quite made it to the champion's crown. He is still an outstanding personality in British motoring.

There is no shame in this. For most of the Fifties, Moss was pitted against the Argentinian, Fangio, who was very nearly old enough to be his father. In 1955, they were team-mates as Fangio drove to his third world championship. Fangio was a brilliant driver who won his first Drivers' Championship at the age of 40 in 1951, and his last in 1957. No-one else has ever won five world championships: Niki Lauda, Sir Jack Brabham and Jackie Stewart would all win the drivers' crown three times, but Fangio was very special indeed. He was a brilliant driver, but he was also a gifted wheeler-dealer, switching teams

as one finished its winning streak and another began it. In 1955, Moss scored what in retrospect is seen as his greatest victory, not at Le Mans, nor in a Grand Prix, but in the gruelling long-distance road race, the Mille Miglia. It was perhaps the one time in his whole career when everything went right from beginning to end.

Mercedes quit motor sport at the end of the 1955 season, a year when they had won the championship for the third time but also suffered Pierre Levegh's tragedy at Le Mans. Fangio went to the Lancia-Ferrari team for the 1956 season, Moss to Maserati. Lancia-Ferrari was the more competitive team, and there was a new young number two for Fangio in the shape of another Briton, Peter Collins. Collins finished third in that year's Drivers' Championship, Fangio first, and Moss second again.

When this tough competition was going on at the very top of the Grand Prix tree, with Maserati and Lancia-Ferrari contesting the honours, things were starting to happen for the British motor racing teams. Previously they had been uncompetitive, but during 1955 something happened. A young British dental student called Tony Brooks, who had had some good drives for Aston Martin, was offered the chance to race a Connaught in the Syracuse Grand Prix. Connaught was cash-starved and Brooks inexperienced, but he went out in practice and set the second-fastest time. Then came the race itself. The Italian Musso, in a Maserati, led, but only for a short while. Brooks, in the traditional British racing green, caught up and passed him, and went on to win. It was the first win by a British car in a Grand Prix for 32 years and it changed matters for ever, not just for Tony Brooks, but also for British motor sport.

Brooks raced a number of times in 1956, and so there were four Britons contesting Grand Prix honours. By that year, a new force was emerging in the sport: Vanwall. It was the first British tailor-made racing team to compete with any chance of real success against the established continentals. The brainchild of Tony Vandervell, whose Vandervell Products made engine components, the Vanwall was a winner. During the 1957 season, Stirling Moss switched to the Vanwall team, with

Brooks as his number two. Moss, as usual, was second in the Drivers' Championship — again to Fangio — but for the last time, because the next year the great Argentinian retired.

1958 should have been the year of the British but in retrospect it was a tragedy. The Vanwalls were very nearly all-conquering, with Moss winning the Dutch, Portuguese and Moroccan Grand Prix races and Brooks winning the Belgian, German and Italian. But Hawthorn in the Ferrari won just enough personal points to deny Moss the championship, so while Vanwall won the first-ever World Constructors' Championship, Hawthorn took the drivers' crown. Collins, the gentle and good-looking driver, won the British Grand Prix in his Ferrari but crashed and was killed during the German Grand Prix at the Nurburgring. A few months after winning the Drivers' Championship, Mike Hawthorn had his fatal accident.

And then there were two. The following season, a new British team was on hand to challenge the Ferraris — Cooper-Climax. Moss flitted between the Cooper-Climax team and BRM, missing out on victories, while a rugged Australian called Jack Brabham stuck to his Cooper-Climax and raked in the points. Brabham took the title with Brooks a narrow second in the Ferrari. Brooks might have won the title himself if he had not taken time off to check the car after a minor collision in the US Grand Prix. Moss, lacking the points, came third. In 1960, another Brabham victory, with Moss third again, this time because of a dreadful accident in the Belgian Grand Prix at Spa in which he broke his legs and injured his spine. He was racing again six weeks later but though he won that race, he could only make third in the championship.

The next year, it was a similar story. By now, Brooks was drifting out of Grand Prix racing; he had had two bad smashes himself and seen too many friends and rivals killed and injured. Moss raced for the new Lotus team which used Climax engines, but they could not compete that season with the Ferraris. Moss won two of the races, the German Grand Prix at the Nurburgring and the Monaco race, but could again only get to third place in the championship. Racing British cars had once more failed to pay off.

On Easter Monday 1962, I watched Moss's career come to an end in a horrific crash at Goodwood. He received dreadful injuries and was forced to quit the sport. No British driver had tried harder to win the championship, and though he never wore the champion's crown, Moss wrote himself into legend. 'Who do you think you are . . . Stirling Moss?' was the question asked time and again by traffic police as they ran speeding motorists to ground, and the phrase lingers on. Moss was the first great British professional racing driver. He realised that to win you had to adopt firm standards, both with yourself and your team. It is significant that his greatest moments came when record-breaking — with the Jaguar at Montlhery and with the MG EX181 record car at the Bonneville Salt Flats — and when racing his Mercedes in the Mille Miglia; all events where he had more than a hand in the running of the organisation. Maybe he lacked the ability to recognise when to switch teams, maybe he tried too hard to get that little extra bit of performance from teams that were not up to it. Whatever the reason, he remains a hero.

While Moss, Brooks, Hawthorn and Collins were racing, a new breed of British racing driver was making its way up through the ranks. During the next decade, men like Graham Hill, Jim Clark, John Surtees and Jackie Stewart would stamp their names on to Formula One racing. Between 1961 and 1971, Britons would win the World Drivers' Championship no less than seven times. Most, if not all of them, would acknowledge the debt they owed to the British drivers of the Fifties.

At home, those who were interested in motor racing made their way to the new race circuits which had opened up after the war — often using old wartime aerodromes as a basis. Goodwood and Silverstone were two popular venues, as was Aintree, where the cars ran inside the famous Grand National course. There was racing, too, at Crystal Palace in south London. A race track called Brands Hatch, near Dartford in Kent, was becoming increasingly popular.

▶Stirling Moss in the white helmet and 'the Boys' at Bonneville Salt Flats in 1957, after a series of record-breaking runs in the MG EX181 record-breaker.

A new era was also dawning for British holidaymakers who wanted to drive their cars abroad. A company called Silver City Airways inaugurated what it called the first regular car-ferry air service across the Channel on 13 April 1949. It used Bristol Freighter aircraft with huge bulbous noses that split apart to allow cars to be loaded inside. The planes flew between Lympne in Kent and Le Touquet, and cars were carried for the sum of £27, if no more than 14 feet long, £32 if over. The price included four passengers and luggage, and the company started flying four services each way every day. The flight took just 20 minutes, with the lumbering Bristol Freighter reaching an altitude of a few hundred feet above the Channel, and then sinking down to land again on the other side. There had never been a faster way to cross the Channel. In 1987, with no aircraft ferries, the fastest route — by hovercraft — still takes longer, and it is doubtful that the Channel tunnel will be any quicker. So much for progress!

Progress of another kind was much slower to arrive in Britain. Despite my father's efforts in the Twenties, Britain still had no motorways, and the arterial roads of the Thirties had become overloaded. Britain desperately needed an up-to-date road system. In 1948, Labour's Transport Minister, Mr A.J. Barnes, proudly announced that the government hoped to bring in a motorway system. The first section, the Preston by-pass, just eight miles long, was finally opened ten years later! After that, progress was gradual; in 1959, the first part of the London to Birmingham motorway, advocated in the Twenties, and indeed suggested in 1903, was declared open. It took until 1986 before the British motorway system could be described as even three-quarters complete, with the opening of the final section of the M25. Over the Channel, our friends in the EEC have developed their motorways and particularly ring roads much faster. German economic revival would not have been possible without their pre-

A gendarme and passengers look suitably impressed as the Silver City Airways Bristol freighter disgorges its cargo of cars in 1949. It was then the fastest way to the Continent, and nearly forty years later no ferry system can equal its original speed and convenience.

A preview for journalists attending the 1952 Motor Show at Earl's Court of the latest creation to be built to the orders of Norah, Lady Docker, wife of the Daimler chairman. No expense was spared and the cars became the talk of the town!

war autobahns, and in the Fifties they were widening and rebuilding their motorways before we had even planned ours. No wonder Germany was able to achieve its economic miracle, and no wonder Germany is today the dominant economic force within the European Community.

There were some wonderful motor cars built during the Fifties by the Daimler company, in what would be its dying spasm. The businessman Sir Bernard Docker, gained control of Daimler and ran it alongside his Birmingham Small Arms

(BSA) group. Sir Bernard had a quite remarkable wife, Norah, Lady Docker. When she was not outraging Monaco with her behaviour — she was once banned from the Principality for an alleged insult to Prince Rainier — Lady Docker tried her hand as a car designer. The more ornate the better, she reasoned, and so at successive London Motor Shows at Earl's Court more and more bizarre creations on the Daimler chassis were displayed. Most cars had chrome-plated brightwork, but Lady Docker wanted hers to be gold-plated — and so it was. Zebra-hide upholstery was specified on one show model: another had hundreds of gold stars laboriously hand-painted on to its sides. The Daimler stand attracted spectators by the score but the new designs did little to delight the company's traditional customers. At about this time the Royals ceased driving in Daimlers, preferring

Rolls-Royces instead for state occasions. Daimler tried to make smaller cars to compete with the Jaguars and Rovers, and failed; tried to make sports cars against the Jaguars and Aston Martins, and failed; and tried to make limousines to beat the Rolls-Royces and failed. In 1956 there was a change of management, but it was too late, and in 1960 Jaguar took over the Daimler company. Jaguar could do everything a bit better for a lot less, and despite the great Daimler heritage, and the royal connection, the company and its products were doomed in time to become Jaguars in all but name and radiator grille — although I still drive one to keep up tradition.

At the other end of the motoring world there was crisis, too. In 1953, the corrupt and tottering monarchy of King Farouk of Egypt had been overthrown in a military coup led by General Neguib. The following February, Neguib himself was ousted by Colonel Nasser. This did little to interest the British man in the street, but within a few months Nasser was making threatening noises towards British interests in the Middle East, and those interests hinged about the Suez canal. The canal was Britain's link with its oil-wells in Persia and its imperial duties in the Far East. Eventually, Prime Minister Anthony Eden decided that intervention was the only possible policy, and in 1956 a combined French and British force invaded Egypt.

At home, it brought back petrol rationing, something the British thought they had seen the last of in 1950. Ten gallons a month was allowed, and in despair, many drivers turned to bubble cars. These were cars in miniature, normally using motorcycle or motor-scooter engines to drive a lightweight body, with minimal accident protection. The bubble cars — BMW Isettas, Messerschmitts, or British versions like the Gordon and the Tourette — sold in just enough numbers to infuriate one senior member of the British motor industry, Leonard Lord. Lord ran BMC, the new company that had been created after the merger of Austin with Morris. He called in the remarkable Alec Issigonis — the man who had created the Morris Minor — to do something about them. The result was the Mini, the British car that revolutionised world car design and passed

into the English language, and which is still produced today.

Issigonis and his team produced the prototype Mini within six months of starting work. It was startlingly different: for a start, the car had front-wheel drive, while every other car being built in Britain had rear-wheel drive; its engine was set across the front of the car, east-west instead of north-south like every other British car; it used rubber suspension instead of the normal metal springs; it was just ten feet long. Leonard Lord drove the first car around the Longbridge factory site for five minutes and then got out. He told Issigonis and his team to have the Mini in production within a year.

There have been all kinds of arguments about the Mini, not least over the inept pricing policy which meant that few versions of the car ever made much money for the company. Some experts contend that the first five million Minis never made a penny. But it did make many more people go motoring, and it made motoring in the Sixties tremendous fun.

Two other events occurred in the motoring world during the Fifties that merit attention. The first was the attempt by the Rover company to adapt gas turbines for use in motor cars; with enormous skill and effort, a gas turbine was slotted into the back of a Rover chassis, and a glassfibre body perched on top. The results was JET I, the world's first-ever gas-turbine car. It caused a sensation, as well it might. The shape of the world was changing: the RAF had abandoned its propeller-driven fighters and bombers in favour of jet propulsion, and here it seemed was the car maker going the same way. Other versions followed, but Rover could never quite overcome the problems of fuel consumption, noise, vibration and heat. At the 1956 Motor Show, Rover exhibited a four-seater coupé with four-wheel drive using the gas turbine. It stole the show but was never going to be a contender for production. Rover's final effort with the gas turbine would come nearly a decade later.

The second event is something much closer to home, indeed my home, and I was closely involved with it. It was the decision to set up the Montagu Motor Museum at Beaulieu, as a means

▲The world's first gas turbine motor car, the Rover Jet 1 being driven out for a test run. The gas turbine car was an interesting idea but never caught on.

◄Peter Ustinov is chauffeured by his official driver in the familiar *Romanoff and Juliet* in a BMW Isetta bubble car. These cars became popular during the petrol crisis of 1956 and it was to counter their threat that BMC commissioned the Mini.

of preserving what remained of Britain's motoring heritage, and presenting it to successive generations. We first opened to the public in 1952, the idea caught on, and more and more cars, motorcycles and other relics found their way to Beaulieu. Among them was the famous bright-red 1,000-horsepower Sunbeam in which Henry Segrave had become the first man to top 200 miles per hour. Ever since the Museum opened, first as the Montagu Motor Museum, later as the National Motor Museum at Beaulieu, the crowds have flocked to it. If ever I want a proof of the passion of the British for the motor car, all I have to do is to look out of the window!

131

REBELLION AND THE MINI

You could do almost anything in a Mini: the film *The Italian Job* proves the amazing car was capable of flight as well!

In no time the Sixties blasted the Fifties into a grey memory. More than any other decade before or since, the Sixties seemed to buzz with excitement. It was a decade associated with revolt, upheaval and change. If you were young, had talent and were British, then the Sixties belonged to you. A young fashion photographer set aside his camera for a few months, married the Queen of England's sister, became the Earl of Snowdon but kept his Mini! A rather scrawny Cockney youngster, Lesley Hornby, proved that being somewhat underfed was no barrier to a modelling career, and took the name of Twiggy around the world. Carnaby Street in Soho became a Mecca for fashion followers and curious tourists. Boutique entered the language, to be followed rapidly by discotheque and a host of other new words.

It was a decade that attempted to realise a multitude of fantasies, most strikingly through the medium of the cinema and television screen. On television children could watch a series of puppet adventure shows that propelled Fireball XL5, and Stingray on to the screens. Then the puppet-master Gerry Anderson created the English milady, her futuristic, six-wheeled pink Rolls-Royce FAB1, and Lady Penelope and the 'Thunderbirds' were *Go!* Grown-up fantasy was well-catered for, too. 'The Prisoner' TV series with Patrick McGoohan opened each week with a Lotus Seven being driven at speed across an airfield. 'The Avengers' brought perhaps Britain's most stylish spy-catchers on to the screens and into the living rooms. It was never quite clear whether or not Steed and Emma Peel were involved off-duty, but on parade together they were magnificent. Steed, with his armoured bowler, his suits with velvet trim and the umbrella that could be used as a deadly rapier, drove a 4½-litre Bentley. Mrs Peel made a grown man's leather fantasy come true, as clad in hide from head to toe she rocketed about in a Lotus Elan.

Cars got steadily more alluring in the Sixties and nowhere was this more obvious than in the

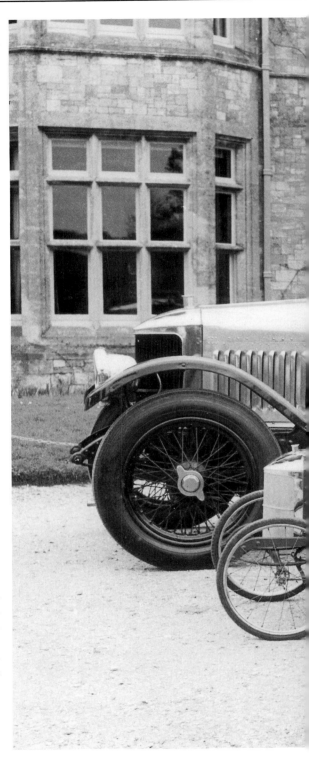

My son Ralph strikes a suitably elegant pose in his model Prince Henry Vauxhall at Beaulieu in the mid-Sixties. I am at the wheel of the full-sized model!

Two bright young things of 1960 pose with the latest model TR3A from Standard Triumph. It was a far cry from Sir John Black filling his pipe in the Yorkshire Dales with the old Vanguard.

136

Above The last days at Brooklands: within months, the once great racetrack had closed for the Second World War. It did not re-open. By 1939 Brooklands was worn out: today a few sections of the old track survive, and the Brooklands Museum is actively engaged in preserving what remains.

Below The War meant all sorts of problems for motorists: petrol rationing was imposed, and efforts made to run cars on gas. They had tried the same idea in 1917. Note the headlamp mask on the other car, for driving in the blackout.

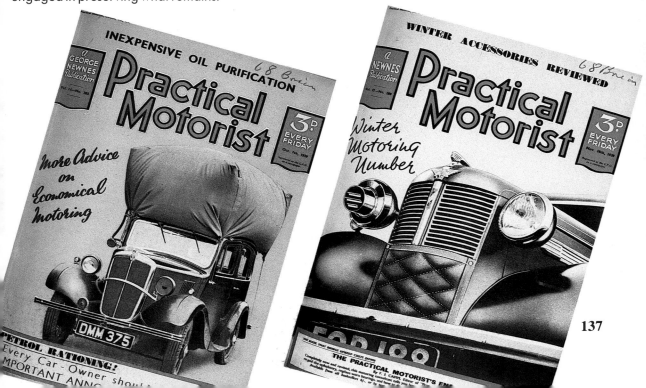

LES 24 HEURES DU MANS 1954
PROGRAMME OFFICIEL

Prix : **200** francs

In the 1950s, the British returned in force to Le Mans, although in 1954 Jaguar could only manage a second place. At home, Ford won more and more friends with its range of cars, while in 1958 Vanwall became the first British firm to win the newly-created Formula One Constructors' Championship.

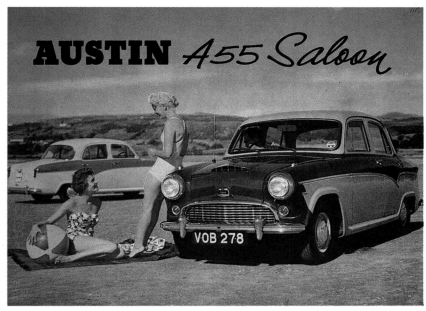

AUSTIN *A55 Saloon*

How the British car industry sold their cars in the Fifties! The girls on the beach with their beachball and the A55 must have sold many a car, though I doubt the sea air did much for the A55's bodywork. In 1959 the world shook as the Mini roared. Sir Alec Issigonis' famous car was known at first as the Morris Mini-Minor, a long title for the little Mini.

WIZARDRY

ON WHEELS

THE
REVOLUTIONARY

"QUALITY-FIRST"

MORRIS
MINI-MINOR

A pride of Jaguars! *Top left*, the 1937 SS100. *Top right*, the XK120 of 1950. The SS title was dropped after the War, for obvious reasons. *Bottom left*, the legendary Jaguar D-type racer, which won Le Mans three years running, and *bottom right*, the beautiful E-type.

From the sublime to the ridiculous and back again! In the Sixties all sorts of things were done to motor cars, and this is John Lennon's own Rolls-Royce, finished in psychedelic colours. *Below*, the oddest car the UK motor industry ever produced, the extraordinary Peel P 50.

Below The Bluebird record breaker of Donald Campbell, captured here so well by the great motoring artist Roy Nockolds.

Above The Austin Healey 3000 has become a classic car of the age, and today commands high prices.

142

Above, the new Jaguar XJ40, which has gone into the Jaguar model line up as the new XJ6, Jaguar Sovereign and Daimler saloon models. *Below*, the latest racing car from the Coventry firm.

The way forward: this is the MG concept car, the EXE. Note the drag-cheating lines and the electronic dashboard, with digital readout. This is the sort of car we might see in production in the 1990s.

Bond movies. M's top agent could not be expected to pootle about in a Morris Traveller or a Ford Zephyr, so for *Goldfinger* Aston Martin went to town, equipping an Aston with machine guns, tyre slashers, a bullet-proof screen and sundry other bolt-on goodies of which the motoring establishment might not have approved. A toy version of this car was produced and it was a sell-out. The debonair playboy might have a Mini for convenience, but in reality he wanted an E-type or an Aston.

During the Sixties, the AA stopped saluting its members, the Mini gave rise to a whole family of front-wheel drive cars and a new short skirt, and parents suddenly discovered the 'generation gap'. More and more Britons poured on to the roads, started to go in their thousands to Spain for their holidays, and became consumers. Young men like Graham Hill, Jim Clark, John Surtees and Jackie Stewart started winning Grand Prix events and championships. In 1964 Donald Campbell took on his father's mantle and regained the land speed record for Britain in new, modern Bluebirds with Bristol Proteus engines. Successive governments realised that Britain really did need to have a decent road system, but faced with balance of payments crises, runs on the pound and devaluation, they did too little, too slowly. And though British cars sold throughout the world, reaching the million-plus mark in 1963, the industry was about to enter the long nightmare that would lead to the troubles at British Leyland.

Britain had once again entered an era of cheap cars, and it was perfectly possible to acquire a 'banger' for £25 or less. True, the brakes might not work, the steering might be more than suspect, the tyres bald and the lights blown, but it was still wheels. In the spring of 1961 the Ministry of Transport test had been brought in to get the worst examples off the road, and not before time. Nevertheless, car ownership extended steadily, and more and more people had the benefit of a car for travel, for shopping, for school and for work.

Central to the motor car explosion and to the decade itself were the Mini and the mini. Indeed, it is no exaggeration to say that the Mini car ushered in the Sixties, and the mini-skirt gave it

character. No picture, TV programme or feature film of the Sixties was complete without Minis racing about with girls in mini-skirts inside them.

The Mini begat the 1100, the 1300, the Maxi, the Moke, the 1800, and in time, cars like the Metro and Maestro of the Eighties. The mini-skirt gave rise, or perhaps the reverse, to the midi and the maxi, and then in a revival of the display-almost-everything-theory, to the hot-pants of the late Sixties.

The Mini was a common factor, though it is not entirely clear whether Alec Issigonis anticipated a new system of society in mind when he designed it! Issigonis was born in Smyrna in 1906, where his family made boilers. He came to Britain in 1921 and went to the Technical School in Battersea, becoming an engineer. He spent time in a design office, moved to Humber and then in the Thirties to Morris. Here he designed the famous Morris Minor which gave such service to so many motorists after the war, and continues to do so even now. The Mini, though, was his greatest creation.

He always argued that he was not a stylist but an engineer. Practicality, he insisted, dictated the shape of a motor car, and since he was patently so brilliant and so adamant about his principles, he was given a more or less free hand. Early Mini owners complained there was nowhere provided in the car for a radio. The reason was simple: Issigonis did not like radios, therefore his car had none. Today, computers are fed with all sorts of information, data, rules, regulations, marketing plans, margins, sales graphs, emission restrictions and the like, and thus come up with cars for different manufacturers that look surprisingly similar!

Issigonis got his own way and sometimes did not get it entirely right. Early Minis showed an extraordinary tendency to take in water whenever it rained, making driver and passengers travel with wet feet: something was evidently not quite right. Eventually it was found that a seam at the rear

▶The expansion of car ownership in the Sixties was unfortunately not reflected in an improvement in the roads. These patient Britons are sitting in a five-mile jam in Kent.

George Harrison's psychedelic Mini outside his home in Surrey. All the Beatles enjoyed cars and Paul McCartney's Hispano Suiza is at Beaulieu.

of the car was the wrong way round and that was cured. The Mini's engine frequently died in the wet because the distributor was exposed too readily to the elements at the front of the car. The need to put this problem right ate into the slim margin of profit on each car.

Despite such faults, however, the Mini caught on, especially with the Chelsea set in London, who realised the little car could be parked on a sixpence. Once you owned one, you had to have those little extras. Lord Snowdon fitted his Mini with a wind-up window on the driver's side, though the sliding windows were retained on the passenger side to avoid discommoding Princess Margaret's hair! Centre consoles were built, remote gear-changes offered, switches made available with extra long levers, even roof-level extra dashboards with provision for more controls and levers and dials. Next, someone had the bright idea of sticking basket-weave on the doors and so everyone wanted it. More lights, furry trim, extra-grip rally seats — all were made for the Mini, and the person who kept his or her version absolutely standard was looked upon with scorn and surprise.

There were freak Minis and Mini freaks: several bits of Mini were welded together to make a Mini 20 feet long; another was welded widthways to make an extra wide Mini; all different Mini options, like the Riley Elf, the Wolseley Hornet, the Mini Cooper, the Mini Countryman with its absurd little wood trimmings; competitions to see how many people could be squeezed into a Mini (33 is the record, but this is no longer published in the *Guinness Book of Records* as it is considered to be a dangerous activity) and then competition proper.

The front-wheel drive gave the Mini tremendous roadholding; with tuning, and protection for the low-slung engine and integral gearbox, to say nothing of the car itself, it was obvious that the Mini could win prizes, especially in rallying. So BMC took the little car onto the rally circuit and very soon it started winning. In fact it was good at most types of motorsport: not fast enough for Le Mans, of course, but devastating in rally-cross, a sport that grew in TV popularity in 1963, when the dreadful winter axed the racing season. Good, too, in saloon-car racing, where its efficient

power-to-weight ratio and front-wheel drive enabled it to dance around the bigger cars. But in rallying it was supreme, winning the greatest of all long-distance rallies, the Monte-Carlo in 1964, 1965 and 1966, only for the cynical French authorities to strip the car of its last victory on the trumped-up lighting technicality in a move that soured Anglo-French motorsport relations for years. The next year, BMC took the Minis back and won the event all over again!

There are many famous British motorists associated with the Mini, but perhaps the man with the greatest obsession for the little car was Peter Sellers. He was the international comedy star who could, it seemed, play anyone and everyone, so long as it was for laughs. The Mini appealed to him and so did the special coachwork that Radford's would carry out to his design. By any stretch of the imagination, Sellers was a car fanatic and bought one Mini after another. He once advertised his Rolls-Royce for sale with the headline, 'Titled Car wishes to dispose of Owner'! He always wanted that little bit extra from life, and with the Mini, he could have everything he wanted. One version had a hatchback, another the original wickerwork panels. Inside, leather and walnut trim, picnic tables, you name it, it had it. The price was beyond belief: up to eight thousand pounds on top of the ordinary Mini. But Sellers had something different!

It was inevitable that the Mini would one day become a film star, and in *The Italian Job,* it did. The last 20 minutes, with the Minis nipping in and out of tiny squares, through houses, main sewers, across weirs, down flights of stairs and eventually into the back of a coach are among the best bits of car film ever shot. So it was that the film's main star, Michael Caine, became linked in his turn to the Mini legend.

While all these delights were going on, other cars were being sold. BMC were persevering with their range of cars, normally available in Austin, Morris, Wolseley and Riley guise, like the Austin Cambridge, Morris Oxford, Riley 4/72 and Wolseley 16/60. They had the A40 too, which used the same engine as the Mini in an orthodox manner, and the evergreen Morris Minor, now the Morris 1000. At Ford they had not been idle

Peter Sellers unwraps his new present to himself by driving a special Mini out of the wrapping paper at Radford's. Britt Ekland is the lady on the dais.

The first of millions, the new Ford Consul Cortina in 1962. The horse looks suitably impressed.

either, and in 1962, they brought out the Ford Cortina, eventually to become legend as Britain's best-selling car for years almost beyond count. The Cortina, too, was used for motor sport, especially when fitted with a beefed-up engine and called the Lotus Cortina. But it would become more famous over the next two decades as the typical company car, issued to salesmen and women, representatives and middle management. Only the Cortina would feature in a poem by the then Poet Laureate, Sir John Betjeman. No other car would do!

One of Prime Minister Harold Wilson's more interesting experiments was to appoint a woman who could not drive as Minister of Transport. Mrs Barbara Castle found herself tackling the problem

of motorists drinking before driving. Alcohol was seen increasingly as a major cause of accidents, and so Mrs Castle and her colleagues introduced the breathalyser. 'Blow into this bag, would you, sir', became a familiar phrase on the lips of Britain's traffic police, though the legislation itself took years to sort out and has required constant updating ever since. In fact, some now argue that the breathalyser has never really worked, because the fact that it is set at a certain ratio of blood to alcohol — or breath to alcohol — implies that the driver can have some measure of drink. As we know now, for some people even one drink in the

Poodle fanciers? Well anyhow this was how BMC sold their cars to ladies in 1961.

system can impair judgement and contribute, if not cause an accident. But the breathalyser did start to eat into road accident statistics.

Cars were becoming more safety-conscious, too. The new Rover 2000 demonstrated a system whereby it was almost impossible for the driver to be speared in the chest by the steering column coming into the car in the event of a crash. The engine, too, would be deflected downwards on impact, rather than into the passenger compartment. The new car was a dramatic change from the Rovers of the Fifties, and it was bought in large numbers by the police force, remaining

a favourite ever since. At one Motor Show in the Sixties, the Triplex glass company, who had worked so hard to develop the laminated windscreen for cars, actually showed a Rover with a full glass roof panel. It did not catch on, but sunshine roofs, so common in the Twenties and Thirties, started to be fitted to an increasing number of cars.

It was a time of British technological advance. The planned Anglo-French Concorde was under way, and Vickers was putting the finishing touches to the new VC10 airliner at its factory at the old Brooklands racing circuit. What could be more natural for BMC than to use the track and the plane as the backdrop for their new MG 1100? The 1100 and 1300 were one step up from the Mini, and capable of holding a family in some comfort. They were the natural successors to the family Morrises and Austins of the Thirties. The Mini required a certain approach and dedication: small might be beautiful, but hopping in and out of an 1100 was a lot easier than squeezing into the Mini.

In fact, one of the unexpected demands the Mini created was a need for small models. Any good-looking girl who was less than five foot two was much in demand for Mini publicity shots. Seated inside, she would make the car look spacious and comfortable. Outside, she would make the car seem less of a toy, more of a proper means of transport. The tall, elegant models of the Eighties would have looked very odd indeed, contorted into the back seat of a Mini-Cooper!

As the Sixties progressed, the sexual revolution exploded. 'All you need is Love,' the Beatles had wailed, and many took heed. Car adverts became more explicit, and the Motor Show at Earl's Court on press day featured many an attractive girl, scantily clad, posing on the manufacturers' stands.

The photographers swarmed round to get the shot and the public followed in droves, at which point the girl always mysteriously disappeared! TVR and Aston Martin seemed particularly keen on having girls on their stands. The model June Palmer started it off in the early Sixties; the DB6 featured a Penthouse Club girl very nearly exploding out of her dress; and by the time the 1970 car appeared, two girls were used, one with just a few strands of metal chain to cover her. It was curious why the British motor industry needed these adjuncts to their sales.

One man who joined the ranks of British motorists was the Prince of Wales. He passed his driving test in April 1967, and a week later was

If you cannot fly the plane, fly the car. A left hand drive MG 1100 with white-walled tyres. Two girls pose beside a new VC 10 at Brooklands.

to be seen in a Rover 2000 on the way back from the theatre. He was the fifth generation of the House of Windsor to become a motorist, and a very enthusiastic one, too. In fact, Prince Charles, Princess Anne and the Duke of York have all taken to motoring with enthusiasm: the Prince of Wales owns an Aston Martin Volante convertible; Princess Anne for years patronised Reliant Scimitar GTEs; and the Duke of York is often seen driving a Jaguar XJS. If they ever have any trouble with the cars, they can always ring up their cousins, the Kents: the Duke of Kent is President of the AA, and his brother, Prince Michael, is President of the RAC and a Trustee of the National Motor Museum.

The Sixties were perhaps the last decade where motor racers could be seen having fun. In the Seventies and Eighties, big money, sponsors, marketing and PR persons have come to dominate what is now very big business indeed. In the Eighties, it is doubtful whether the British man-in-the-street can recognise more than one of Britain's four current Formula One stars. In the Sixties, Britain's four different world champions were instantly recognisable and loved — perhaps because they did not allow themselves to be drawn too much into the merging media machine, perhaps because they won championships.

The longest-established and the most familiar of the four, was Graham Hill. He had come up through club racing in the Fifties, racing of all things, an A35. He got together with Colin Chapman and his Lotus team, worked with them while the team established itself in Formula One, and then joined BRM. In 1962, he won the World Championship with BRM, and was runner-up for the three following seasons. One of the men he had to keep trying to beat was Jim Clark, a Scot; Hill was a Londoner who raced in a helmet painted with the markings of the London Rowing Club of which he was a member. Clark joined Lotus as Hill left, and fought his way to the top,

collecting the World Championship in 1963. Two British victories on the trot — which of them would win next year? The answer was neither!

Clark was a quiet, softly-spoken man: Hill, a wisecracker, nearly always exceedingly charming. The third British world champion of the Sixties was a friendly, though rather quieter, individual called John Surtees. He was a world champion on two wheels before he was ever a racer on four, but he went on to win the Formula One Drivers' Championship, thus becoming the first and to date the only man to have won World Championships in both sides of the sport. Surtees took over the British post-war pre-eminence in motorcycle racing from Geoff Duke, and was world motorcycle champion four times between 1956 and 1960. Then he switched over, winning the Isle of Man TT Race one month and taking second place in the British Grand Prix a month later. Hill and Clark knew they had a fierce competitor on their hands, and in 1964, with a Ferrari, Surtees beat Hill to the championship by a single point.

Yet amazingly, there was a fourth British champion on the way: another Scot. Jackie Stewart joined BRM from a similar background to Clark; Clark's family farmed in Berwickshire, Stewart's ran a garage in Dumbarton. Stewart had been a crack clay-pigeon shot before he ever became a motor racing driver for Ken Tyrrell in Formula Three. He prospered mightily by applying the highest standards to his racing, and then was offered the chance to join Lotus as number two to Clark, or BRM as number two to Hill. He chose BRM, and finished third in the championship season of 1965. Hill was second, Clark champion.

There was a pleasant informality to these great stars. In 1965, Clark, Hill and Stewart were photographed having a wild time on the dodgems at Butlin's holiday camp at Bognor Regis. Today it would be difficult to get three Formula One drivers together for five minutes in public without an attendant crowd of hangers-on, minders and fixers, let alone on the dodgems at Butlin's. In the Sixties and Seventies, the tradition of a cricket match was founded after the British Grand Prix in which both drivers and journalists took part. Today, they head straight for their helicopters and word-processors respectively. There is no time for

◄Aston Martin trying their own approach to the Spirit of Ecstasy at the Motor Show in 1968. There was a vogue for this sort of exhibit at the time.

155

cricket, or any form of public relaxation for the top drivers.

Between 1962 and 1971, British drivers won the Formula One Championship seven times, and were runners-up six times. No other country has ever dominated the sport so thoroughly and convincingly — but there was a price to be paid. Jim Clark died when his Formula Two Lotus crashed at Hockenheim in Germany in 1968. There were no crash barriers and the tiny car smashed into a tree. Graham Hill, by then his Lotus team mate, won the World Championship almost in tribute. The next year, Hill broke both legs in a crash at the US Grand Prix, but returned to driving. Stewart won the Championship that year, the first of his eventual three victories. Hill eventually drifted away from the front-line teams and formed his own. He formally retired from driving in 1975, planning to concentrate on his team and its brilliant young driver, Tony Brise. In the winter of that year, they flew home together after testing the car at the Paul Ricard circuit in the south of France. Hill was piloting his own light aircraft. They crashed near the airfield at Elstree, and he, together with Brise and other members of the team, were all killed.

Surtees, too, tried running his own team, but it was not a great success. He could not find a driver with the same skill as his own, and the morale of the team never seemed high. The cars were not competitive and Surtees more or less gave up driving in 1971. The team stayed in being until 1978 when he decided to call it a day. Stewart turned out to be the luckiest of the four: he won the World Championship three times, demonstrating brilliant skill and a totally professional approach (as Stirling Moss had done a decade earlier). He then retired from racing and went into business, winning lucrative deals with Ford and Goodyear, to name but two. Today, he is a multimillionaire businessman and friend to Royalty, displaying utterly professional marketing skills despite the handicap of dyslexia and spends much

'If you want to be world champion, Jackie, you have to take a big size in boots!' Graham Hill offers advice to the No. 2 B.R.M. driver.

Jim Clark, Graham Hill and Jackie Stewart and friends carving each other up on the dodgems at Butlins! This was a happy era in motor sport.

time promulgating road safety all over the world. A single meeting is enough for Stewart: his encyclopaedic brain recalls name, role and character in the same way he used to sum up a new car, tyre or race-track. Meet him again after a number of years and he will instantly recognise you and pick up the conversation where he left off. Quite a skill!

While the four British musketeers were stamping their mark all over the dangerous world of Formula One racing, one Briton was pitting himself against the loneliest battle in sport — Donald Campbell. The Sixties was the time when land speed record cars were starting to change. Previously, they had all been cars based on the same principle as an everyday motor car: the engine driving the wheels through some form of gearing system. Now people were trying for the land speed record using jet engines strapped onto a chassis: a sort of wingless aircraft, or jet-propelled roller-skate. Campbell decided to go about it the old way. Despite a horrific crash at Salt Lake, he took the repaired and beautiful Bluebird to Lake Eyre in Australia, and in the shimmering heat of the Australian desert, raised the record to over 403 miles per hour. It was an achievement deserving the highest praise and reward, but a few weeks later, an American achieved a greater speed in a jet-propelled car. The Europeans recognised the Campbell record,

The boy and the man: (*Inset*) Donald Campbell poses with a model of his father's Bluebird in 1931 and does up his shoes prior to taking his own Bluebird out on the sands of Lake Eyre in 1963.

the Americans wondered what they were arguing about, but Campbell's record stands as the last one achieved by a wheel-driven car. In 1967, Campbell was killed, going for the water speed record on Coniston Water, the third of Britain's speed kings to die in this way. The modern Bluebird car survives as a tribute to his bravery, skill and tenacity, one of the four land speed record cars at the National Motor Museum. I am very proud that it has a home with us at Beaulieu, and as the Museum has grown, these cars have remained overall the most enduring attraction to visitors.

Thus, the Sixties gave us huge changes in style and in sport. One never knew quite what would happen next, and so much of it happened around motor cars and the British: Graham Hill, doing what no other man has ever done, winning the Formula One Championship, the Le Mans 24-hour race and the American Indianapolis 500; the all-conquering British rallying Minis; the Hillman Hunter rally car which won the London to Sydney marathon rally of 1968; British racing teams triumphant in the Constructors' Championships, year after year. But perhaps the image of the Sixties which will remain is that of swinging London, and Lord Snowdon, George Harrison, Peter Sellers and the rest, zooming around town in their Minis. The age of rebellion was the age of the Mini.

159

The MG Midget: a car of charm, but axed by Sir
Michael Edwardes.

Whereas the Sixties seemed delightful because of their unpredictability, the Seventies appeared dull by comparison. There were still heroes: James Hunt on the racetrack brought a cheer wherever he went, with his informal mode of dress and ready smile. Yet in some ways he was a child of the Sixties anyway, and still is today. The flair for design had swept past the British motor industry: during the Sixties they had been able to claim the Mini and the other BMC front-wheel drive cars, but the Mini was an engineer's achievement, not a designer's, and the rest of the family was starting to look quite old by 1970. Instead, the British motor industry began to produce some unimaginatively designed cars and lose its share of the market. Soon BL would require massive pruning to make what was left remotely viable. And by that time the British motor industry had lost much of its domestic base. How the mandarins of the Thirties and Fifties must have been horrified by Sir Michael Edwardes' assertion that BL needed 20 per cent of its own home market as a minimum. In the 1950s, a marketing executive had shocked his bosses at one of the car import firms by suggesting that overseas firms would one day have much more than ten per cent of the British car sales market. He suggested 30 or 40 per cent was not impossible. Today it runs at just over 50 per cent (1986 figures), with Japanese importers limited voluntarily to around 11 per cent.

Other British domestic manufacturers, including Ford and Vauxhall, had always been able to cater for their own market. In the Fifties there had been import restrictions and long waiting lists for new cars. As the restrictions eased and the long consumer boom began, foreign cars were seen as something rather exotic and fun. They were more expensive to run and maintain, but there was a style about them that the British did not attempt to copy. Then the Japanese, who had previously wiped out the British motorcycle industry, turned their attention to our car market. They made good,

The Royal Family continued to be loyal patrons of the British Motor industry in the Seventies. Here is Princess Anne behind the wheel of her sporty Scimitar.

Two very positive elements to come out of the Seventies: crash-testing and the increased use of the breathalyser.

inexpensive, reliable cars, with a high standard of specification. The British car industry, hit first by the oil crisis, and all the time by worsening industrial relations, lost its competitive edge. The Consumers' Association began to produce regular reports on cars' reliability, and often BL cars were at the bottom of the list. In time, Ford and Vauxhall were able, with their world-wide base, to pump in investment and restore credibility, but for quite some time in the Seventies, they too were struggling to be reliable.

The Seventies also saw a strong move in favour of safety. Efforts began in earnest to make the wearing of seat-belts compulsory. I moved a successful amendment in the House of Lords

A sign of the times at the height of the oil crisis in 1973-74.

which at that time failed to come to fruition because of the impending general election. The MoT test was tightened up. The brake firm, Girling, started to offer free check-ups for drivers. Windscreen washers improved from little pump arrangements (or even rubber bulbs let into the dashboard) to fully electrically-operated, factory-fitted standard equipment. Rear wipers sprouted on the hatchback doors of many cars. There were efforts to reduce the dangers of punctures, with tyres which would run flat if need be. High-intensity rear lamps appeared, at first linked to

165

the brakes, later on a separate switching system linked into the main lighting. Halogen bulbs replaced the old-style filaments in headlighting, and dual-circuit brakes, disc at front, drum at the rear, with servo assistance, became commonplace.

This was the era of the Volvo 'Tank', when the Swedish firm started selling cars with big bumpers. It was the decade when more and more cars underwent rigorous crash testing during development, rather than as a final test of acceptability to the authorities. Designers looked to raise the safety of car occupants as safety was starting to sell cars: families bought child and baby seats to secure youngsters when driving. In fact cars could be sold on the strength of their 'safety-cage'.

In 1973, after one of the Arab-Israeli conflicts, the countries in the Middle and Far East, Central and South America who depended on oil as their major export, formed the Organisation of Petroleum Exporting Countries — Opec. The Arab embargo made Opec a household word in Britain, and it caused panic and confusion. The price of oil for industry went up and up, and so did that of petrol. Furthermore, with the embargo, motorists thought they might not get any fuel and many panicked. Long queues formed outside petrol stations to get extra fuel and delays of up to an hour were commonplace. Some garages ran dry, others limited buyers to a couple of gallons or turned away all but account customers. The government realised there was danger in all this and prepared to reissue petrol coupons. Meanwhile, the miners were readying themselves for the great strike which helped to bring down Edward Heath's Conservative Government. A combination of that strike, electricity power cuts, the three-day week and two general elections in one year, plus high petrol prices and the fear of short supplies, made British motorists very much aware of the need to make a gallon of petrol go that bit further. Across Europe, they had the same idea, and so fuel economy became a vital priority for car designers and salesmen.

It was not the sort of background which would lead to exciting motor cars being built: safety on the one side, fuel economy on the other. Nothing wrong in either concept, but as a basis for design,

it was constricting. Buyers looked at cars with big engines and said 'no'. There were fears that companies like Jaguar, then part of British Leyland and suffering quality problems, could be in serious trouble with its large engines. Who would buy a V-12, 5.3-litre car, with petrol shooting up in price? Thankfully, the Jaguar management held its nerve, which means that in the Eighties we are still able to enjoy cars like the XJS.

A new word started to be used in relation to cars: aerodynamics. It was a science that was little understood, either by the public or by the car makers. Wind-tunnels had been used to help design cars before, but soon it was realised that not all the car makers had the same sort of wind-tunnel, nor the same sort of measuring equipment,

The Rover 3500, voted 'Car of the Year' in 1977.

nor the same design notions. It therefore took some time before a series of measurements was agreed that would establish drag coefficients common to all motor manufacturers. The move towards aerodynamics was accompanied by sudden research into lighter materials. Soon the car designers were experimenting with the same sort of composite fibres being tried out by aircraft manufacturers and racing car teams. By the Eighties, cars would be available with bonnet panels made of man-made fibre, and towards the 1990s, it looks more and more likely that whole cars will be made in new materials.

Safety, in the form of crash-testing, front and rear seat-belts, child and baby-seats, safety cages, rear high-intensity lights and the like was wedded to fuel economy: making that gallon go further by reduced performance, different gearing and reduced speed limits that so many countries including Britain adopted in the wake of the oil crisis. Lower motorway speeds meant longer hours behind the wheel for the rep and salesman in his Escort or Cortina. Fatigue means danger, and longer hours put stress on individuals, helping to induce rear-mirror paranoia. But many people pointed to what they saw as increased motorway safety and lower fuel consumption, and Ministers largely supported their view.

The media must take some blame for what

167

happened to motoring and the British motor industry in the Seventies. Fleet Street seemed to take a lugubrious satisfaction in reporting every dispute, every stoppage, every go-slow in the motor industry. Even in the mid-Eighties, many British motorists still do not believe that Austin-Rover can make as good a car as the Japanese or the Germans. The fact is that many Austin-Rover cars are better, cheaper and more reliable. But persuading the public of that is likely to take many years of hard work.

Britain still made great cars. The new Rover 3500 was voted 'Car of the Year' by an international jury in 1977. Ford's Escort and Cortina, in their many different guises, continued to dominate the best-seller lists in Britain. No other country made a vehicle quite like the Range Rover. But throughout the industry there were problems with reliability and delivery. It was during the Seventies that the luxury German car makers, BMW and Audi, really began to get a grip on the markets, as Jaguar and Rover failed to provide everything that the customer wanted. In many ways, the Seventies proved what the Fifties had shown: without restrictions on the supply of cars, the buyer would choose what the buyer wanted. The customer would always be right.

The industry's failure was mirrored in motor sport. Jackie Stewart was still winning championships at the start of the Seventies, but when he retired after winning his third Drivers' Championship in 1973, things began to go downhill, at least as far as Formula One was concerned. Between 1974 and 1986, Britain produced just one world champion: James Hunt. The Ulsterman, John Watson, managed a third place in the championship in 1982, and Nigel Mansell was runner-up in 1986, but that was that. The nation which had dominated motor sport in the Fifties and Sixties was suddenly nowhere. At Le Mans it was the same story. No named British manufacturer seemed interesting in fielding a truly competitive team, and any British driver worth the name had normally to look elsewhere for a drive. People like Chris Craft and Alain de Cadenet tried very hard but they were up against formidable opposition from the German Porsche company, which had realised the benefits that

could accrue from success in sports car racing. In the Seventies, British drivers won Le Mans just three times: Dickie Attwood in a Porsche in 1970 partnered by a German, Graham Hill in a Matra-Simca in 1972 with a Frenchman, and Derek Bell with Jackie Ickx of Belgium in the only British car to win the race that decade, a Gulf-Mirage. The British national car makers did make one effort to win in sports car racing during the Seventies but it was not a success. Leyland thought it might boost flagging fortunes by entering Jaguar Coupés in saloon-car racing as part of the European Touring Car Championship. The cars looked marvellous and the crowds turned out in force to watch them race. The trouble was, the cars kept on losing and breaking down. *Autosport* described the whole project as one of 'unremitting failure'. Hundreds of thousands of pounds had been spent without a single victory.

One of the few British racing drivers to make it through the barrage of popular newspaper prejudice was James Hunt. In many ways he resembled the sort of young Englishman who became the mainstay of the Bentley team at Le Mans in the Twenties. Well-educated, well-connected, good-looking and charming, he was full of fun with an ability to raise hell at short notice. On the other hand, what might have suited during the age of frivolity was not quite what was needed for the mood of the Seventies. The same reaction that had set in amongst the car makers had affected the racing teams. Big money was starting to flow into the sport, turning it from competition into mega-business. Now the drivers' lives were becoming increasingly dominated by the agent, the accountant, the travel agent and the sponsors' timetable. Jackie Stewart, with his extraordinary professionalism, adapted well to the new serious sport. James Hunt, eight years younger, was much less restrained.

He had a rather bad start to his career, winning many races, but wrecking many cars. 'Hunt the Shunt' he was called behind his back in the race game, and sometimes to his face. With millions of pounds riding on every team, managers and sponsors seemed reluctant to take on this 'enfant terrible'. What he needed was a fairy godmother, and he got it in the unlikely shape of Lord Hesketh.

Alexander Hesketh and Hunt were about the same age, Hesketh had money, and he wanted to go motor racing. He was rather too large to do it himself so he set about organising his own racing team. In 1973, the team, with its teddy bear emblem, entered the Race of Champions using a hired Surtees car, and Hunt came in third. So Hesketh bought a car, this time a March, and they raced it against the might of the other Formula One teams all over Europe, culminating in a second place in the US Grand Prix. That was quite an achievement in itself but Hesketh went one better: he decided to have his own team cars instead of buying them, and designer Harvey Postlethwaite built the first Hesketh racing car. They did not manage to win a Grand Prix in 1974, but the following year they won the Dutch. That

One of Britain's greatest motoring designers, Sir Alec Issigonis at work, just prior to his retirement in 1971. His cars continued to sell right the way through the decade.

was a great triumph and the champagne flowed, just as it had throughout the Hesketh team's history. They were a tiny race team, but they could win a Grand Prix, and they knew how to enjoy themselves.

At that point, Lord Hesketh realised he could not afford to continue pumping money into motor sport, and when searches to find a suitable sponsor failed, Hunt moved to McLaren Racing. It was the kind of move that Fangio used to make in the Fifties, and was just as successful. Hunt started winning, getting high places and challenging the existing world champion, Niki Lauda, in his

169

Ferrari, every inch of the way. There were rows and disqualification in the British Grand Prix, and in the Spanish, appeals and reinstatement. Even the popular newspapers began to realise that something was going on. Lauda pulled ahead in the championship, only to crash and receive terrible burns at the Nurburgring during the German Grand Prix. A British driver, Guy Edwards, stopped and pulled him out, but to the world, Lauda was finished, apparently dying in hospital having been given the last rites. Hunt found himself against the South African driver Jody Scheckter, McLaren against Tyrrell, and everyone thought that would be the way the championship would be decided. But six weeks later Lauda was back, swathed in bandages, horribly scarred, and racing again. He finished fourth in his first Grand Prix since the crash, while Hunt failed to finish. Lauda was set for a second championship.

It looked very bleak for James Hunt, but then his luck changed again, winning two Grand Prix races, and finishing third at the Japanese Grand Prix to take the championship by a single point from Lauda. James Hunt was world motor racing champion for 1976, and there has not been a British champion since. Three years later, he retired, returning to Formula One as a commentator. It is a role which suits him: together he and BBC commentator Murray Walker have forged an unusual but never unfunny relationship: Walker, hectic, excited, delighted, amazed: Hunt, dry, urbane and laconic. Many people watch the BBC televised highlights of Grand Prix events not so much for the cars, as for the interplay between the two men at the microphones!

While Hunt was racing in Formula One, another British star was emerging. Derek Bell, the Sussex farmer, has proved to be a complete natural in a sport which has changed dramatically since the Fifties. Long-distance sports car racing used to be based around the great Le Mans race, now it is a major championship in its own right, with endurance races being held around the world. Bell's story really belongs to the Eighties, but

Britain's world motor racing champion, James Hunt, in 1975 — with that characteristic naughty grin.

suffice it to say that during the Seventies he — with other British drivers like Guy Edwards, John Fitzpatrick and David Hobbs — was notching up wins and awards in a sport that is every bit as demanding as that of Formula One.

One of the most exciting developments in the Seventies was the growing enthusiasm for older cars. Just after the war, it had been possible to buy cars, like vintage Bugattis, for a couple of hundred pounds. Even in the Fifties, the price for older vehicles stayed fairly low. Many cars vanished into the breakers' yards and were never seen again. The Montagu Motor Museum in the Fifties tried to preserve what remained of Britain's motoring heritage, and to pay tribute to pioneers like my father. The interest was proven by the crowds who flocked to see the film *Genevieve*, loosely based on the London to Brighton Veteran Car Run, and who then turned out in droves to see the film's other 'stars' — a 1904 Darracq and a 1905 Spyker.

We were very heartened by so much interest in the great cars and the pioneers of the past, but the depth of that nostalgia had not fully developed then. Accordingly, in 1956 I bought a magazine called *Vintage and Thoroughbred Car* and relaunched it as *Veteran & Vintage Magazine*. Circulation trebled in the first year, and more and more people came to Beaulieu to see the cars, lorries, buses, vans, motorcycles and bicycles we had assembled. Through the Sixties more and more enthusiasts acquired their own cars. This led to price increases for the old cars until, in the Eighties, the most important examples fetch thousands and thousands of pounds. In 1986 a Bugatti Royale fetched $8.1 million at auction. Ever since 1960 when we had Britain's first old car auction at Beaulieu we have not missed a year, and the auction is now conducted in association with Christie's. For old cars to be treated like fine art and given the same aura of respectability in the auction room may seem very strange. At least the high prices paid for the best cars mean that some of the more ordinary old vehicles have become worth saving.

During the Sixties and Seventies, one-make car clubs abounded. The Bentley Drivers' Club, of course, is a long-established organisation, as are

171

Prince Charles and Earl Mountbatten in 1975 inspecting the 1901 Columbia Electric Car which once belonged to Queen Alexandra, Prince Charles' great-great-grandmother.

the Veteran Car Club and the Vintage Sports Car Club. A typical specialist car club is the MG Owners' Club, which emerged from a few adverts in the *Exchange & Mart* to become a rival to the existing MG Car Club, and catering for the owners of all MGs, but in particular the MGA, B, and C, plus the modern MG Midget. As BL would shortly close the MG factory at Abingdon and end traditional MG sports car production, this was good timing and no bad thing!

While the old car movement — the veteran, vintage, post-vintage thoroughbred and classic market — was forging ahead, so too were the do-it-yourself car owners. There had always been motorists who preferred to do their own car repairs and maintenance, and with increasingly stiff

standards being set by the authorities, it was important for the home mechanic to ensure his car was in proper working order. Many developed a taste for it, and were never so content as when busy taking their cars to bits. In fact I am sure they enjoyed that side of their motoring far more than driving their cars, even when they actually put them back together! There was a boost in the number of magazines and periodicals devoted to do-it-yourself motorists, plus an equally big lift in car maintenance guides produced for individual makes and models of cars. By the time these were added to the existing motoring magazines, the cars' section of most newsagents' shelves was packed to overflowing!

To many, the 1970s was a decade of BL. It was born out of a hotchpotch of companies, a monster that might have worked and did not. There were two halves to the monster: the first the Leyland half, the other the BMC. BMC comprised the great names of Austin, Morris, Wolseley and Riley; Leyland and the great bus and lorry-making company itself, plus Standard-Triumph. That was at the start of the Sixties. The Standard name was dropped as being meaningless to the modern buyer, and in the middle of the decade BMC acquired Jaguar, and Leyland picked up Rover. In 1968, the two huge bits were brought together to form the British Leyland Motor Corporation, and what a jumble it was! The company made and sold cars under no less than nine different names — Daimler, Jaguar, Rover, Triumph, Austin, Morris, Riley, Wolseley and MG — and they owned the rights to many more. They had cars that competed directly with one another for sales, cars which had totally different design bases, and parts — engines, gearboxes, axles, suspensions, brakes, steering — which were not interchangeable. Their component suppliers stretched the length and breadth of the country. On top of that, they had inherited designers and engineers from all the different firms, each with his own idea on making cars. Marketing and sales people found themselves working with, but still against, colleagues who had until recently been deadly rivals. PR men had to find common ground with one another, as did the senior executives who had come in from the various divisions. And that was just on the cars' side! There were bus and truck people too, and experts in commercial vehicles from the Leyland and BMC sides to be welded together.

It was obvious that the hydra-headed monster had to be sorted out and streamlined. Suppliers had to be brought into line with the new system, the workforce severely cut, and plants needed to be shut down and production transferred. However, that was not to be allowed by the Government: Labour, which had given birth to British Leyland, had not done so just to see Labour voters losing their jobs. The problem lasted right through the Seventies, with the further embarrassment of the Leyland Cars Jaguar racing team just one public example of the way the system was not working. At one stage, the famous Jaguar works in Coventry was reduced by the Rayner Report to be known as 'Large Car Plant Number

One'. Anonymity for the factory which had built the C and D-Type Le Mans winners! No wonder quality suffered. Steadily, the government took a greater hold on the firm as its stock crashed and it cried out for cash. The city was unwilling to provide funds, investors shied away and so the government had to step in. It was in 1977 that command of the ship which was well on its way to becoming a submarine was entrusted to Michael Edwardes, a businessman born in South Africa who had made a brilliant career with the battery makers Chloride. He now took centre stage as he tried to revitalise the company.

Edwardes saw no point in continuing with the present situation and started a policy of cutting back. The project which would have led to the replacement Mini, the ADO88, had already been cancelled before he arrived. Edwardes decided that the company would need a new small car, bigger than the Mini, but able to make money. He therefore went ahead with the project that became the Metro, launched in 1980. Meanwhile, factories needed to be closed, and the Speke plant on Merseyside, which built the TR7, was shut down, just as a new drophead version of the car was launched. Production was switched to Canley in the Midlands, but did not last very long after that. Edwardes decided to close the old MG works at Abingdon, and despite attempts to keep the name alive, the doors shut. Having started with two sports cars — the TR7 and the MG — Edwardes now had none. Realising that BL needed to buy-in technology, Edwardes initiated talks with the Japanese, which would eventually lead to the BL/Honda tie-up, and the series of cars which have resulted from it.

While life at BL continued to be eventful, Ford ruled the roost with its two first-rate cars, the Escort and the Cortina. BL could not match their sales, nor could Vauxhall until it developed the front-wheel drive Cavalier. Ford of Britain were so prosperous, that for one year they were able to support their American parent when it ran into trouble. Ford had their own industrial relations

▶ The MGB: like the Midget it is now virtually a collector's item.

problems too, but they seemed slight when viewed alongside BL's.

And just as the serious Seventies ran out, a new figure appeared on the scene. He had once been the rising star at General Motors, now he intended, with help from the British Government, to build a futuristic, stainless-steel sports car in a brand-new factory in West Belfast. Unlike Puerto Rico and the Dublin Government, the British did not turn down John Zachary DeLorean!

▲The new boss at British Leyland: Michael Edwardes.

▶Sir Terence Beckett poses when chairman of Ford of Britain with four different versions of the long running Cortina.

176

In 1986, the motor car attained its one hundredth birthday. It deserved to be a year of celebration, recording the many benefits that the motor car has brought to mankind since those first horseless carriages built by Karl Benz and Gottlieb Daimler in the Neckar Valley back in 1886. For the great German car firm, Mercedes-Benz, it was indeed a centenary, since that company was the result of the merger of the Benz and Daimler companies in the Twenties. Accordingly, they celebrated in grand style, but the rest of the world was rather muted in its applause. True, the car had brought about all sorts of benefits to all sorts of people, but it had also brought problems.

From humble beginnings, with the gentry scoffing at the spluttering, greasy, dirty little machines, the motor car had grown to become the single most important means of transport in the world. By the Eighties, there was not a family living in Britain or indeed the world who had not benefited from the car at some time or other. More and more people owned cars: in 1984 it was estimated that more than 17 million motor cars were in use, and one and a half million commercial vehicles. More and more people could drive: in 1984 around 25½ million Britons had full or provisional driving licences. It is interesting to compare those figures with the pioneering motoring years in Britain in the late 1890s. Then, the number of cars in Britain could be counted merely in hundreds. How the car had changed too! In the very early days it was little more than a cart or carriage with its yoke and harness removed. Now it has developed far beyond the imagination of the early pioneers. My father visualised the round-London Orbital Motorway, the London to Birmingham motorway and other trends years before they arrived, but I doubt if many of the beginners could have thought of electronic ignition, anti-lock brakes, automatic transmission, micro-processor controlled dashboards and instrumentation, air-bags or on-board computers. They would have been amazed by the electronic diagnostic servicing now possible on many cars,

and staggered by the computerised traffic lights that keep traffic more or less moving in central London and other great cities. They knew that the motor car would one day be taken seriously, but to imagine a Britain where almost half the country's population could drive would have probably been inconceivable.

Production methods, of course, have changed dramatically. Consider the modern assembly lines at Ford, General Motors, or at Austin-Rover's plants at Longbridge and Cowley. Instead of thousands of men and women using their bare hands, nuts, bolts, a welding torch and a needle to put cars and their upholstery together, we now have row after row of robots, guided by laser and controlled by computers, swinging back and forth in great showers of sparks to make complicated individual welds on parts of car bodyshells as they move automatically down the line. The machine never needs a lunch-break, can't catch 'flu, and does not need holidays. The grimy overalls for the assembly workers have gone: many now wear white coats, carry clipboards and concentrate on keeping the robots and the computers running to peak efficiency. The workers have become technicians of the robot age. The cars have reached infinitely greater heights of reliability and of quality in construction than would have been possible even a decade ago. New materials are being used. Instead of hundreds of seamstresses working till their hands bled to make seats and interior trim, machines exist which can make and shape headlinings and the foam inserts for the seats and the covers to fit them. There are far fewer jobs in the motor industry itself than there used to be, but those jobs command a far higher rate of pay and offer more satisfaction. Conditions have improved beyond recognition; employees can enjoy the sort of cleaning and washing facilities that formerly only the bosses enjoyed, and return home clean, tidy and refreshed.

The same is true for the drivers and passengers in the cars that the new factories produce. There is no reason today for anyone to travel in a car in discomfort. Seats are designed to fit the human body, and the materials used leave the passenger feeling not too hot, nor too cold, nor clammy, but just right. There are no draughts from ill-fitting

◄No 'U' turns for Mrs Thatcher — and certainly not on this final section of the M25 which was opened in October 1986.

doors or windows. Car heating and ventilation has become a science in itself; companies like Saab pass all the air which will be used in their ventilation systems through a filter which removes even the microscopically-small particles of pollen that cause hay fever. Firms like Jaguar, Mercedes and Rolls-Royce have developed air-conditioning systems that maintain a constant climate of clean air within the car; you can set the Rolls-Royce system to two temperatures, one for face level, the other for feet. Set the car in the far north of Norway, drive to the south of France, and the temperature will stay exactly the same. You arrive at your destination fresh and relaxed.

It is even possible nowadays to drive for hundreds of miles without ever touching the accelerator. Many cars now have cruise-control systems which are fitted on a lever on the steering column. It will accelerate or decelerate the car at the driver's whim, and hold a constant speed on motorways better than the human driver ever could. A touch on the brake disengages the system instantly . . . but touch the control again and the car resumes at the speed you set. To prove its efficiency, one motoring writer recently drove from Exeter to London via the M5 and M4, and used the brake pedal ten times, the throttle just twice.

The component which has brought all these recent sweeping changes about is the microchip, a tiny piece of electronic hardware which thinks faster than a human mind, and takes up a fraction of space. The chip, in all its forms, can help to make a car, design a car, order the parts required and replacement supplies for them, arrange the buying of the car, its licensing and its delivery to the customer. The chip helps start the car, assesses the various control and electronic circuits automatically and then provides a warning to the driver if anything is wrong. On the road, the chip keeps a watchful eye on speed and fuel economy, and makes the driver's task simpler and safer.

Yet all the benefits of the humble chip, both to the motor industry and to the driver and passenger, have not brought about a new wave of affection for the business of motoring itself. The car is no longer the same prized possession it once was. Few drivers go out every Saturday morning

lovingly to polish and clean their beautiful machine: they run it through the car wash instead. They curse the crowded roads and fight to get through the rush-hours with a savagery that would have appalled the early pioneers. Those pioneers stopped to talk whenever they met another car: modern motorists stop in surprise and amazement when they find themselves on an empty road devoid of other vehicles. They also spend much of their motoring time jammed in traffic instead of actually moving.

To the general public the motor car was initially seen as a nuisance, then as a joy and a blessing, now that blessing is looking very mixed indeed. Pollution and congestion are the two main causes, and as we become more environmentally conscious, the dangers of the motor car have become more apparent. It was the Americans who first noticed that the car in great numbers presented special problems; the car-loving Californians realised that the smog which formed over their city of Los Angeles had something to do with car exhaust emissions and they took steps. Then the successive oil crises made us all realise that the oil in the ground which we turn into petrol is a finite commodity and society started to frown on cars that guzzled gallons of fuel. The Nordic countries and the West Germans saw that their trees were starting to die in great numbers. The cause was atmospheric pollution, known as acid rain, which was aggravated by car exhausts. Britain, by the Eighties, had become a leading member of the European Community, and when the Brussels experts decided to deal with car emissions, Britain had to follow suit. It was realised at home too, that the car was obtrusive! More cars were coming on to the roads, and the roads were not built to cope with such numbers.

The Eighties have shown an ever-increasing emphasis on ambition and consumer need. Nowadays, three out of every five cars bought in Britain are bought for business, or by businesses. The role of the company car would represent an important part of a history of motoring in the last twenty years. It is no longer the perk of the senior manager or the essential tool of the rep. Cars are given as part of the job and as part of the job's remuneration. With pressure being heaped on an

181

ever-increasing number of people in the work-place, small wonder that it results in aggressive driving and anti-social road manners. People are less careful of their cars than they used to be, and less concerned about other road users. Cocooned in their motor cars, they are remote from each other. They feel they are more or less safe: it is unlikely that another driver will try to remonstrate, and accordingly all the worst aspects of driver behaviour shine forth. Add the continuation of some badly designed roads to such arrogance and false security, and is it any wonder that accidents occur?

Perhaps that was why the EEC decided that 1986, the centenary of the motor car, should be European Road Safety Year, the year in which all member countries of the European Community should do something to make their citizens aware of the potential dangers of road usage, and to seek ways of reducing the accident statistics. In Britain, the Department of Transport concentrated its anti-drink drive message for Christmas 1986 under the slogan, 'If you drink and drive, you're a menace to society'. Friends, relatives and business colleagues were urged to keep an eye, and a restraining hand, on one another's drinking. If you went to the pub with a friend for a drink, and he was driving, the idea was to make sure that he did not drink alcohol. If you were having a dinner party, you did not force wine on your driving guests. Rather the reverse in fact. The aim was and is to change attitudes among the British motorists of the Eighties, along the lines of Sweden where drink is totally restricted as far as driving is concerned. Time alone will show if this sort of approach works. In another development, companies started sponsoring road safety. The great Scottish insurance company, General Accident, decided to put two million pounds

►Daimler still retain the same classic lines nearly 100 years on from their first car. Here is my 4.2-litre Vanden Plas.

▲►Sir Clive Sinclair demonstrates his ill-fated C5; despite the relatively cheap retail price of £400 the machine never caught on. There was some alarm that it was legal for 14-year-olds to drive the vehicle without a licence.

182

towards investigations into accidents and driver behaviour. Up till now, British firms have only been interested in sponsoring charity, sport or the Arts — fine things of course in themselves — but with the General Accident move, it is to be hoped that more companies will follow its example.

The 1980s brought us all sorts of motoring developments. The DeLorean car was a disaster. Others were more successful. In 1980, BL unveiled the car to save the company: the Metro. It received good press coverage. Yet some of the articles tended to deal with the car, not on its own merits, which were excellent, but on its relevance to the future of British Leyland. In fact during the Eighties, BL has ceased to be a giant and is now just a national car company, smaller than the American or Japanese corporations.

The Metro's most famous owner was the former Lady Diana Spencer, who used her little car to get to work from her home in Clapham. The Metro and Lady Diana were suddenly projected into the public gaze when her name was linked romantically with that of the Prince of Wales. All at once, Lady Diana could not get into her car without attracting the attention of a huge flock of photographers and reporters. No commuter has ever been so famous overnight! The Metro was a life-saver for BL: it was followed in turn by the Maestro and Montego, two derivatives of the same development, and meant to help BL's Austin Rover Group recapture some of the mass market lost to Ford and General Motors. The two cars have not been conspicuously successful, and following the appointment of Graham Day as BL Chairman in 1986, the Chairman of Austin Rover, Harold Musgrove, departed together with some of his senior staff. BL's other car in the early Eighties was the Triumph Acclaim, the first car to be built in cooperation with Honda. Cynics sneered at the extent of the cooperation with Japan, declaring all BL was doing was paying a lot of money to make a Japanese car under licence. However, it worked: BL have dropped the Triumph name and used the technology and the cooperation to make the Rover 213 and 216, and have taken a further lease on the Honda tie-up to make the Rover 800. This will be built by Honda in Japan and sold there: in exchange BL are

Product of BL's deal with Honda: the Triumph Acclaim.

making a Honda version of the car to be sold in Britain by Honda as a rival to the Rover 800 range. BL is quickly becoming a part of Japanese world-wide strategy.

Perhaps the best success stories of the Eighties for the British motor industry belong to Rolls-Royce and the Jaguar. Rolls-Royce took a brave decision and introduced the Bentley Mulsanne Turbo as the first Rolls-Royce car to have a turbo-charged engine. It made a very fast car indeed, and the press were delighted with it. Sales for Bentleys started to pick up, and with them the fortunes of Rolls-Royce Motors as a whole. In the early Eighties, they had had to lay off or make redundant many of their staff, but as the Bentley name re-emerged from the shadows, it revived Rolls-Royce's spirits. Great and ghostly names of legendary drivers from the past were conjured up when the new Bentley Turbo was introduced to the press along the great Mulsanne straight at the Le Mans track, where the Bentleys of the Twenties had gained their victories.

One of the new Bentleys of the Eighties which have helped Rolls-Royce motors rebuild their image as 'makers of the best cars in the world', the Bentley 8 in a suitably British setting.

Britain's fourth major motor manufacturer — the French Peugeot group are now building their 309 model in Britain.

Jaguar were pulled out of their downward spiral by a management team led by John Egan, who had previously headed BL's Unipart division. He believed the future lay in the past: Jaguars had always sold well under a policy of providing remarkable value and quality and an unbelievably low price compared to the competition. He concentrated on quality above everything else and suddenly Jaguars were just as good as they had been and better. The cars started selling again, not just in Britain, but in the best export market for British luxury cars — the United States. The Tory Government wanted to take Jaguar out of the BL fold and privatise it. On a wave of popular enthusiasm, with many Jaguar staff taking advantage of their allocated shares, Jaguar came to the market and was an enormous success. Egan pressed on with the quality, keeping development of the planned new XJ40 saloon going until the last possible moment. In the autumn of 1986, it

was launched as the replacement for the existing Jaguar XJ6, and given the same name. It was received with great enthusiasm: one company placed an order for one hundred cars on the day it was launched! For his work at Jaguar, Egan received a knighthood. The chairman of Vickers, David Plaistow, whose companies include Rolls-Royce Motors, has also received a knighthood for his achievements.

There were two other genuinely notable achievements for the British motor industry during the Eighties, the first at Talbot, the second at Nissan. Talbot, part of the French Peugeot-Citroen Group, had inherited the old Chrysler car empire in Britain. In 1986, they decided that the Peugeot 309 hatchback should be built in Britain as well as in France, and production reached such a stage that the company was able to announce that all the Peugeot 309s sold in Britain would be built in Britain. In the old days, this might have affected sales: in 1986 it did not. The same year, the Nissan plant at Washington in the north-east began to produce cars. There had been many fears about the Japanese coming to Britain. Wise old motor industry heads shook knowledgably. This, they muttered, was a new Trojan horse come to Britain. In time, ten thousand jobs would be created in the north-east: the motor industry experts reckoned that those ten thousand would be at the cost of ten thousand elsewhere. The Government was helping a company set up in Britain, when it could spend the same money strengthening the British motor industry instead.

They had ample cause for dissatisfaction on two counts. The first was they had seen the Japanese make big inroads into the UK car market before they were halted by the 'voluntary' agreement between the British Society of Motor Manufacturers and the Japanese Automobile Manufacturers Association. This 'voluntary' agreement had first been set up in the Seventies by Labour's then Trade Secretary, Peter Shore, who asked the Japanese to respect a voluntary limit on their exports to us. There was the implied threat that if they did not do so, there would be a public demand for trade sanctions. The Japanese were asked for an 18-month moratorium, a moratorium which has gone on ever since. Every six months, the two sides meet, talk and play golf together, and in this happy way the Japanese restrict themselves to around 11 per cent of the British car market. It has certainly saved the domestic industry. The Government and the Nissan company then became involved in negotiations to build a car plant here in Britain. Both sides knew that Nissan wanted unfettered access to the European car market, and that the only way for the company to get round the many European restrictions on Japanese goods was to make them here in Britain. Time will tell whether they made the correct gamble, and whether the native British car industry can survive the new competition, but there are now many more jobs in the north-east and there are many British components in Nissan cars.

The second reason for the worry in the UK car industry was the DeLorean fiasco. John DeLorean

The Nissan Bluebird: a Japanese car built in Tyne and Wear.

John DeLorean looking confident beside the sports car that was supposed to take the Eighties by storm. The project failed.

had come to Britain and persuaded successive Governments that he should build a car with taxpayers' support in West Belfast. It was to be no ordinary car. It would have gullwing doors that opened upwards, and a stainless-steel body. There would be plenty of performance from a mid-engined Renault-powered transmission, and the car would sell twenty thousand units a year at a very low price in the United States, Britain, Europe and around the world. It should have sounded too good to be true, but there was a desperate need for jobs in West Belfast. Estimates vary, but around 80 million pounds of grants and taxpayers' money was 'invested' into the project — it flopped. DeLorean had to get Colin Chapman's Lotus company to sort out the car:

when they tested it along the old airfield runway at their plant at Hethel in Norfolk, it is said the gullwing doors came adrift at speed, and flapped up and down like a giant prehistoric bird trying to fly. There were rumours that money had disappeared, and at the height of those rumours, Colin Chapman died from a sudden heart-attack. An Inland Revenue investigation into the DeLorean-Lotus deal went on for months. DeLorean himself took to flying back and forth across the Atlantic and making great noises about more investment round the corner in the United States. Jim Prior, the new Ulster Secretary, was not convinced, and sent in the receivers at the DeLorean plant. Their most famous comment was

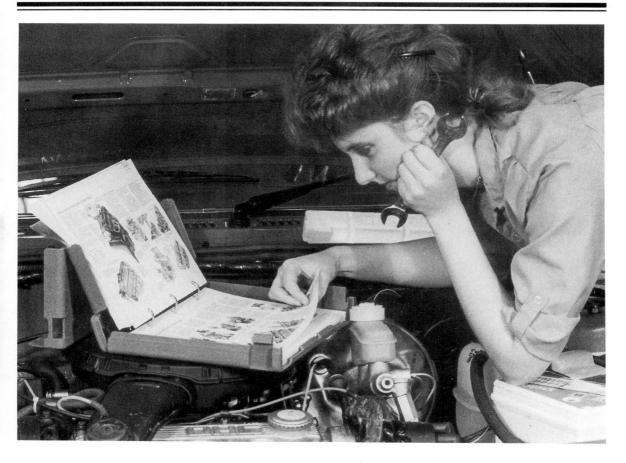

about all that public money which had been pumped into the firm. It had gone 'walkabout', they confided. DeLorean was arrested and charged by American narcotics agents on charges of drugs smuggling, on which he was later cleared. He became a born-again Christian, and thanked the Lord on his acquittal. He still talks of making a car.

If Lady Diana, Sir John Egan and John DeLorean were three of the British motorists of the Eighties, then the two that stand out from motor racing are Nigel Mansell, the Formula One driver, and the world endurance racing champion and four-times Le Mans winner Derek Bell. Mansell was runner-up in the 1986 Drivers' Championship, and was tipped to win but never quite made it, having trouble with a tyre in the last Grand Prix of the season. Mansell is one of several British drivers currently in Formula One:

By the 1980s women had had enough and were doing their own car maintenance: this picture would have warmed the heart of Kitty Brunell!

the others are Jonathan Palmer, Martin Brundle and Derek Warwick. Of the four, Mansell has been the most successful to date.

Derek Bell has specialised in long-distance sports car racing, though he had ambitions towards Formula One, and was once in the Ferrari team. He had made his reputation driving the fastest and most dangerous cars in the world at circuits like Sebring, Daytona, Mount Fuji, Buenos Aires, Mosport, Spa and the Nurburgring, and especially Le Mans. The cars are considerably faster than a Formula One car, reaching speeds of around 240 miles per hour or more on the Mulsanne straight at the Le Mans circuit. Accidents are frequent, injuries and burns common, deaths a regular feature.

Bell has survived this pressure for more than a decade and a half. Partnered with the great Belgian driver, Jackie Ickx, he won Le Mans three times, in 1975, 1981 and 1982: and in 1986, sharing the driving with the German, Hans Stuck, and the American, Al Holbert, Bell took his fourth victory, something no other Briton has ever managed to do. Yet despite this long history of success, he has never become a household name. Nowadays the populist newspapers tend to ignore it. This is a pity because it is still a true sport, full of drama and excitement. Bell remains British sport's best ambassador, immaculate in dress and behaviour, always ready to sign an autograph or pose with a fan for a picture no matter how tired he is. There are many sports personalities who think their duties begin and end with the cameras and the interviews: Bell has always made sure that the fans get their share too.

The Eighties have one more hero, Richard Noble, who made his name not on the racetrack but at the wheel of a great car. When young, Noble had seen John Cobb's Crusader speedboat being taken north for an attempt on the water speed record at Loch Ness. Cobb was killed, but the memory of that boat, and the notion of speed, stayed with the young Noble. When he grew up, he decided he too wanted to break records, and went for the land speed record. Very few companies were willing to invest money, but Noble persisted, raising the money, having the car built and rebuilt, and getting it shipped out to the Black Rock Desert in America two years running to try for the record. Eventually, after weeks of frustration, Noble made the record-breaking runs, achieving 633.46 miles per hour and the land speed record came back to Britain.

While men like Bell, Mansell and Noble were keeping the Union Jack flying in their fields, there were big changes at home. One of the important trends of post-war times has been the ever-growing number of women motorists and car owners. Women now account for an ever-growing share of the UK car market; one in three women holds

Making beauty out of the ordinary car — Ford took the roof off the Escort to make their top-selling Cabriolet.

a driving licence, and that figure is increasing; surveys show that women have a vital say when it comes to buying a family car. The old days of sexist jokes about women drivers have gone, banished to all-male confines. Car maintenance courses for women are packed out, and an increasing number of women are finding their way into the higher echelons of the British motor industry. They have even formed their own charities of which the oldest is the Dog House Club. Another, Women on the Move against Cancer, has recently raised thousands of pounds for cancer-related charities. Women have a greater say in car design, not just in fabrics and trim, but in all areas of research, design and development.

During the Eighties, it became possible to set up a network of tiny transmitter-receiver sites across the UK, linked together like hundreds of body cells to a central computer. The cellular radio system is ideally suited to providing the means for mobile telephones, and with so many business people on the move, car phones make sense for those who need to keep in touch. Typically, development and installation outran the legislators, especially when it came to road safety, and one of the worrying sights of the mid-80s has been to watch motorists in the fast lane of a motorway at 70 miles per hour or more, with one hand on the wheel and the other holding a telephone. The Highway Code states that such phones should only be used when the car is parked or a hands-off system exists for those who must talk to their friends and colleagues while moving. There is now even a phone matched to the driver's voice, which will dial up as many as 20 different numbers on demand. The driver just yells and the phone does the rest.

The Eighties have been full of ambition, and with the increasing power of the consumer, the car makers have come to build cars that their customers actually want. The cars must be safe and secure, reliable and stylish. There is no place for the rust bucket in the Eighties, and cars which have a reputation for rust are shunned by buyers. This is an excellent move, because it has made the car firms more careful of their design techniques and their construction methods. Many cars now come with anti-rust guarantees or warranties. And cars are much more fun, too! Take for instance the Ford Escort. By itself, it is a very good motor car, now offered with an optional anti-brake locking system which is a triumph for the Lucas-Girling and Ford engineers who worked to design and fit it. The little Escort in the Eighties sprouted all sorts of go-faster bits in an option called the XR3 and now the XR3i. These sold like hot cakes to young upwardly-aspiring professionals in big cities, and then Ford produced a soft-top version. The Ford Escort Cabriolet is undoubtedly the best-looking car the company has made since it was involved with the GT40 Le Mans car project back in the Sixties. The GT40s were beautiful sports cars which won the great race for Ford several times, but they were out-and-out racing cars. A very few were made and sold for road use, but nowhere near the enormous numbers of Ford Escort Cabriolets now being built and sold to Eighties customers. Volkswagen of Germany have had similar success with a convertible version of their Golf GTi, and the convertible, thought to be a dying breed ten years earlier as a result of Ralph Nader's safety campaign in the USA, is now back with a vengeance!

All that comes as no surprise to the thousands of motorists who have carried on with their MG sports cars from the Sixties and Seventies. Thanks to their thriving Clubs, MG enthusiasts have kept their cars going, and seen the price for them rise steadily. Along with roadster versions of the Jaguar E-type and drop head Aston Martins from the Sixties, the MGs have become cars to own and cherish. Wind-in-the-hair motoring is still very popular!

In the autumn of 1986, the last stage of Britain's last great motorway, the M25, was finished. Its 117 miles are meant to act as a huge by-pass for the capital, though the streets of London seem still to be crowded. The M25 was originally envisaged as an outer ring road for the capital; there was meant to be another nearer in, plus the inner ring-road. A small section was built in the Seventies, but it was killed off by an incoming Labour administration at the Greater London Council, who campaigned under the slogan 'Homes before Roads'. The homes did not get built but the inner

ring-road was stopped. Today, the M40 Westway, the best piece of road in West London, stands as a memorial to what might have been. Congestion in London gets worse every year, and it is hard to see how it can be eased without a major programme of road improvement, or new inner ring road construction on the lines of the Paris Perifique.

The younger Royals like Prince Andrew and Prince Edward have become active motorists during the Eighties, joining the Princess of Wales, Prince Charles, Princess Anne and Captain Mark Phillips. The Princess of Wales has her own tiny frog mascot on the bonnet of her cars, and is often seen driving in London and Gloucestershire. The Duke of York drives an XJS, and Prince Edward has been seen at the wheel of a Rover. The Royal Family still relies on Rolls-Royces for its official transport: cars are lovingly kept in the Royal Mews, and the Society of Motor Manufacturers and Traders presented Her Majesty with a new

Prince Andrew, still then the playboy Prince, takes the wheel of the Granada in the early 1980s.

Rolls-Royce Phantom VI on the occasion of her Silver Jubilee in 1977. Whichever of the royal cars Her Majesty travels in is fitted with her own mascot: St George defeating the Dragon.

The Eighties still have several more years to run, but they are proving to be very exciting for the ordinary British motorist and there are many imminent new developments. The stresses of modern living have much to answer for, and in the years to come, it will be necessary for car designers, manufacturers and dealers to work very hard with the transport planners and police authorities to make motoring easy and sensible. At the National Motor Museum, we can see the changes in Motoring which have taken place down the years, and the pace of change quickening. What is going to happen in the years to come?

In 1906, the year in which Rolls-Royce were to reveal their new Silver Ghost model at the London Motor Show, and construction of the world's first motor-racing track was to commence at Brooklands, my father John Scott-Montagu, wrote these words:

'What is the future of automobilism? That it will to a great extent replace nearly every other kind of traction upon the surface of the earth, I have but little doubt. That it will help to solve political and social problems but at the same time create others, is equally obvious. It will affect values of land, towns and houses by a redistribution of values. Town houses and sites of all kinds, whether for business or pleasure, are going to become less valuable because they largely depend for their value on concentrated humanity, in other words, on inferior transit facilities. On the other hand, land in the country and on the outskirts of towns and in villages remote from railways will become more valuable because of the greater ease of access.

'Population will gradually tend to become less concentrated and be diffused over wider areas. Travelling in the broad sense will increase enormously, and dustless motorways will be constructed between principal towns to carry the ceaseless traffic which will use them by night and by day. The workmen employed by the new method of transit will in twenty years overshadow in numbers and importance those employed by railways and tramways added together.

'Large towns will have special arterial roads to connect their centres with main roads outside. There will be but little noise, no smell, and, with dustless roads, no dust in the traction of the future. No bacteria will breed in fermenting horse-manure, and the water-cart will be unknown. Produce will come direct from the country to the consumer, and necessaries and luxuries of life will be alike cheapened.

'The cultivation of farming in all countries in which the motor-car eventually prevails will gradually alter; the foods raised for the horse, partly or exclusively, will tend to disappear, for oats, for instance, will not be wanted to feed horses, and more foodstuffs for cattle will be grown, and a greater amount of land will be devoted to the raising of foodstuffs for mankind.

'Another great change which the motor-car will bring about will be the creation of a new kind of internationalism. To this influence the one preliminary condition will be the existence of passable roads. Europe in a few years' time will become for the motorist one vast holiday area, whether he is seeking health, change of scenery, a warmer or a colder climate as the case may be. Hotels, even in anti-motorist countries such as Switzerland, will find the motorist not only the most profitable but the most common source of revenue.

'The country which has the best roads will in future tend to become more and more prosperous, given that its natural advantages are not inferior to the countries which surround it. New countries which are being opened up will no longer build railways, but roads — as was the custom till seventy years ago, before the coming of the railway, and roads will be justly regarded as the necessary hallmark of civilization. Enormous sums will be invested in new road-making and new vehicles all over the world.

'Is this an exaggerated picture, the result of a vivid imagination only, or a prophecy to be fulfilled? Time alone can show.'

Eighty years later, the reader may judge the answer to that question for himself.

The British motorist has come a long way since my father took the future King Edward VII for that famous drive through the New Forest. Indeed, the whole world that they knew has changed, not beyond recognition, but in a manner and at a speed which would have staggered the early British motoring pioneers. They were setting themselves against ignorance and prejudice, challenging years of supremacy of the railway engine and centuries of transport by horse, but could they even have guessed at the world we live in towards the end of the twentieth century? A world where man flies on a daily basis, when space has been conquered, and where electric power is generated by the splitting of atoms. Where the British Empire has

◀ Built from Kevlar, the new TVR 420 S.E.A.C. represents advanced British automotive design.

196

vanished, where Britain herself has become a nation whose international responsibilities and trading links are intertwined completely with 11 other countries in Europe. A world where the motor vehicle reigns supreme, and where cars are in use 24 hours a day.

The world has certainly changed. The motor car has played a vital part, freeing families from the restrictions of public transport, making it possible for friends and relatives and business colleagues to meet more frequently, allowing families to shop, to get to school, to get to work, to go on holiday with none of the complications of a century ago. Yet because successive Governments have failed to anticipate future developments, the car in many parts of Britain creates problems which are difficult to solve.

Most of our great cities and towns were not designed for the motor car, and are difficult to adapt to cope with it, even if the car is changing to meet the demands and requirements. The 21st-century family should not be required to live or work in cities whose roads are clogged by night and day with cars and other motor vehicles expending fumes and creating a cacophony of noise. Within the great cities, like London, new road schemes are essential, to provide urban by-passes and overhead roads and to allow communities to regain their freedom. The construction of new roads means homes will have to be demolished. Years of neglect of roads in the capital cannot be remedied simply or overnight. It is going to cost the country dear, yet without adequate urban roads our cities will surely stagnate and die.

On the new roads, there will be many electronic controls. The means already exist to sense when a road is overloaded and to adjust traffic lights in many areas: in the great cities these will have to be brought together and expanded to cover the entire metropolis. The built-in road sensors and computer links will boost traffic flow, easing congestion and saving time and energy. The same electronic systems will also be applied on Britain's motorways. The heavy traffic which already exists on the M25 will require better information systems in the future. There is no point joining a clogged motorway but this is precisely what happens at present. Drivers should have access to instant road information to make their own decisions whenever possible, or allow the car's own computer brain to do it for them.

Already in Europe, automatic road information — ARI — is a reality. The system works via car radios. Your radio, whether turned on or not will enable you to pick up special broadcasts to warn you of delays ahead. You can avoid danger, turn off the motorway, and above all, avoid stress and irritation by knowing what is going on.

A quicker route towards road information — certainly for motorways — involves the setting up of huge electronic signboards at the side of the road. These warn of delays or dangers ahead and give advice to drivers. They can be controlled from a central police headquarters or activated by police on the scene, using typewriter keyboards linked electronically to the signs required. Yet another road information system is being developed by Philips, whereby the road details of an entire country can be contained in data information form on the same sort of compact discs which are now used in domestic hi-fi systems. Their travel information system acts simultaneously as a map and for guidance. Type out on the miniature keyboard where you want to go, and the system will get you there, giving you left, right, straight on and other instructions as you proceed. It can even be updated to take into account the latest roadworks, accidents and weather conditions. This system was shown to the public at the British Motor Show in the autumn of 1986 at the National Exhibition Centre, and could be available as a factory-fitted option by the early 1990s.

All these developments depend on the ubiquitous microchip in its many forms. The chip is revolutionising transport and the motor car in particular, though the motor manufacturers offer its benefits only on their top-of-the-range models as a luxury extra, which I think is short-sighted. When systems are developed — such as anti-brake-locking — they should be brought in as quickly as possible for the benefit of all drivers, passengers and other road-users. Such an anti-brake-locking system on your luxury car will enable you to stop when a motorway pile-up begins, but it should also

benefit the driver behind, before he smashes into you. That is why Ford must be applauded for offering their latest Escort and Orion models with an anti-brake-locking option. When the government — and presumably the European Community — takes the decision to make such systems obligatory on all cars, then many more lives will be saved on our roads.

The chip is also being used to monitor engine performance and fuel economy. It can do the job much faster and better than any mechanical system, and as pressures mount to make the car a cleaner device, I expect the chip to play a vital role in reducing exhaust pollution. The car's worst faults are pollution of the atmosphere through engine emissions and pollution of the environment through noise and congestion. Cars are becoming

'Man at work', using his newly fitted car phone. Britain is leading the world in the speed of installation of cellular car telephones.

cleaner, helped by new fuels and new emission regulations in Europe, and are also becoming quieter, with sophisticated research and development into engine noise now paying off. The chip has helped in many ways, and if it can also be used to ease congestion, then motoring will be better and safer for all of us.

The drivers of the year 2000 will have cars which are lighter, stronger, quicker and safer than those we use today. They will still run on petrol, though diesel and perhaps electricity will — with present developments — have a larger share of the market. It is probable that a battery breakthrough will enable a genuine electric car to be available for the 21st century. Those motorists will drive along a British motorway system greatly improved, with further improvements and extensions. Already it has become necessary for some of the motorways to be rebuilt and widened. In towns, the car will be taken away from the main streets and centres of community. More High Streets and shopping areas will become places to walk, talk and shop.

Interesting experiments are being carried out whereby a driver will spend every moment of his motoring life over a 12-month period wired up to a set of computer sensors. These will check his pulse, blood pressure and other reactions as he drives, setting them against what the car itself is doing. It should provide valuable information as to the effects of driving on the British motorist, and show where motoring exerts its greatest stresses. Twenty years hence, the car itself will monitor the driver, and show when he is at greatest risk, through fatigue, for example.

One of the more distressing criminal developments of the Seventies and Eighties has been the boom in autocrime. This is a new word, used by police to denote several things. It can be malicious damage to a car, theft from a motor car of goods and possessions inside, or theft of the entire car itself. The Government has asked the motor industry to improve the security of cars, and better locks, for instance, are now being fitted. Burglar and intruder alarm systems are also effective: a person skulking too near a car could be detected by the future security system, and a warning bleeper would sound. At the same time, the driver would be given an audible warning alert on his car key fob, enabling him to return and frighten off the would-be thief, or tip off the nearest policeman if the system was widely developed and integrated.

Future British drivers will not need keys: the motor cars of ten years hence will open by personal sensors. Either the driver will put his fingertips against the sensor, or the device will recognise a card, like a credit card, or perhaps a tiny identity marker in the pocket. The car will open only to authorised users, and when that user steps inside, the car seats will adjust to his weight and height automatically. On cold days, he can alert the car to trigger off a heating system to clear frost off the windows, lights and mirrors, and warm the interior of the car. As he sits down inside, the car will automatically check through all its various systems and report status, either through a voice system or on a screen. The driver will then tap into the computer where he wishes to go and the car guidance system will issue suggested directions.

The driver will be able to issue many of his instructions to the car verbally. Cars already speak to their owners, warning them about seat belts or light failures. In future, the driver will be able to speak back, ordering the lights to turn on, the wipers to commence operation, the screen to be cleaned. The car in its turn will offer advice; sensing the amount of water droplets in the atmosphere, it will conclude that fog is setting in, and suggest to the driver that rear high-intensity lamps might be necessary. In acute cases, the system could ignore the driver and switch the lights on for itself. Man should be able to depend on his car to be an intelligent servant.

Drivers themselves will be better trained and tested. The existing UK driving test is rapidly falling behind those of other countries. I hope soon that, as in the USA, schools will include driver training as part of their curriculum on a national basis. The test itself should fall into two parts, written and practical, and young drivers would have to undertake an advanced test within a few years of first qualifying. Until they passed that test, certain high-powered vehicles would not be available to them. A proper eyesight and medical check would become mandatory before receiving a provisional licence, and drivers' eyesight kept up to the mark by a requirement that periodically they should visit an optician for a check-up. Opticians could have their offices linked by computer to the DVLC at Swansea and could report the result direct to the Centre. As annual eye check-ups are free under the National Health Service, it could dramatically help to prevent accidents if the eyesight standard of Britain's drivers were raised.

There will be further improvements in Britain's breakdown services. Already, computer technology is helping the motorist back on the

Britain's motorways are already wearing out and rows of cones have been a familiar sight for the last decade. By the year 2000 much of our motorway network will have to be renewed.

road. A motorist phones in, perhaps on his car telephone, to report a breakdown. His location is established using no fewer than five levels of computer map to pinpoint the spot. The nature of the breakdown is discussed: the nearest garages and repair specialists brought upon the screen, together with details of what they can do, and the driver could well be on his way within the hour. If the car cannot be repaired, a second car or even a chauffeur-driven car can be provided. In the future, the car itself will detect that something is wrong, alert the breakdown organisation, establish its precise location using the car guidance system linked to the breakdown organisation's computer, and have the appropriate expert on his way to fix the breakdown almost before the driver has come to a halt.

All this is going to demand an even greater leap forward from the car manufacturers. Some of the firms who specialise in the automotive microchip are already ten years ahead of the cars coming into production, and that gap is increasing steadily. To close the gap would entail considerable research and development costs.

What the British motorist of the year 2050 will be driving is pure guesswork. In Germany, Mercedes-Benz have carried out a good deal of research using their Prometheus project. They suggest that future motorists will climb into their car, state their destination and the car will take them there automatically, with the driver having to do nothing at all. The cars of the Eighties will be viewed with as much disbelief, delight and nostalgia as we today regard the pioneering vehicles which take part in the London to Brighton veteran car run.

One thing is certain: the National Motor Museum will go on collecting everything which relates to the motorist and his motor car. We already have on display the cars, bicycles, motorcycles and vehicles from the first hundred years of the motor car and now are planning to preserve and cherish those of the motor car's second century.

The latest product of BL's co-operation with Honda, the Rover Sterling.

INDEX

Page numbers in bold type indicate illustrations